Renal Diet Cookbook for Beginners

Jasmine Patel

100 Recipes with Images, Tips, and a 28-Day Meal Plan for Those with Kidney Disease and Dialysis

The information in this book is not intended as medical advice or to replace a one-on-one relationship with a qualified health care professional. It is intended as a sharing of knowledge and information from the research and experience of Jasmine Patel. We encourage you to make your own health care decisions based on your research and in partnership with a qualified health care professional. You may not be familiar with many of the ingredients listed herein. To help, we've included some basic information for many of the more unusual items. However, please note that some of the ingredients are considered medicinal in nature. So, before consuming large quantities of anything you're not familiar with (or, if you have any special medical condition or are taking any prescription medication), please do a bit of research and/or talk to a medical professional when in doubt.

© Copyright 2024

-JASMINE PATEL-

All rights reserved.

Table of Content

INTRODUCTION 6
DIET FOR THE KIDNEYS 7
FOODS FOR RENAL DIET 10
MEAL PLAN 14
BREAKFAST 20

    Oatmeal with Sliced Bananas and Almonds *21*
    Scrambled Eggs with Spinach and Feta Cheese *22*
    Low-Phosphorus Smoothie (Berries, Apple, Greek Yogurt, and Ice) *23*
    Whole Grain Toast with Avocado Slices and Cherry Tomatoes *24*
    Cottage Cheese Parfait with Pineapple and Walnuts *25*
    Brown Rice Cake with Cream Cheese and Smoked Salmon *26*
    Quinoa Breakfast Bowl with Berries and Almond Milk *27*
    Poached Eggs over Sauteed Spinach and Mushrooms *28*
    Homemade Muesli with Low-Potassium Fruit (e.g., Apples, Pears) *29*
    Greek Yogurt Pancakes with Blueberries *30*
    Chia Seed Pudding with Mango and Coconut Flakes *31*
    Vegetable Omelette with Herbs *32*
    Low-Sodium Veggies and Egg White Scramble *33*
    Buckwheat Pancakes with Strawberries *34*
    Sweet Potato Hash with Poached Eggs *35*
    Cantaloupe and Honeydew Melon Salad *36*
    Homemade Granola with Low-Phosphorus Nuts (e.g., Almonds) *37*
    teamed Asparagus with Soft-Boiled Eggs *38*
    Low-Phosphorus Bran Muffins with Apple Compote *39*
    Tomato and Cucumber Breakfast Salad with Feta Cheese *40*
    Brown Rice Porridge with Cinnamon and Raisins *41*
    Egg and Vegetable Breakfast Burrito with Whole Wheat Tortilla *42*
    Low-Sodium Turkey Sausage with Sweet Potato Hash *43*
    Cherry Almond Breakfast Quinoa *44*
    Spinach and Mushroom Breakfast Quesadilla *45*
    Homemade Low-Phosphorus Scones with Berries *46*
    Cauliflower Hash Browns with Poached Eggs *47*
    Papaya Boat with Cottage Cheese and Lime *48*
    Low-Phosphorus Bran Flakes with Low-Potassium Berries *49*
    Smoked Salmon Wrap with Cream Cheese and Cucumber *50*

LUNCH 51

   Grilled Chicken Salad with Mixed Greens and Balsamic Vinaigrette 52
   Lemon Herb Baked Cod with Quinoa and Steamed Broccoli 53
   Vegetarian Chickpea and Spinach Curry with Brown Rice 54
   Tuna Salad Lettuce Wraps with Cherry Tomatoes 55
   Eggplant and Zucchini Lasagna with Ground Turkey 56
   Salmon and Asparagus Foil Packets with Lemon 57
   Mediterranean Chickpea and Vegetable Bowl 58
   Turkey and Vegetable Stir-Fry with Quinoa 59
   Shrimp and Avocado Salad with Lime Dressing 60
   Roasted Vegetable and Lentil Soup 61
   Caprese Chicken Skewers with Basil Pesto 62
   Cauliflower Rice and Black Bean Bowl with Salsa 63
   Spinach and Feta Stuffed Chicken Breast with Roasted Brussels Sprouts 64
   Quinoa and Black-Eyed Pea Salad with Herbs 65
   Zoodle (Zucchini Noodle) Primavera with Grilled Chicken 66
   Low-Sodium Minestrone Soup with Whole Wheat Bread 67
   Baked Sweet Potato with Kidney Beans and Salsa 68
   Sesame Ginger Tofu Stir-Fry with Brown Rice 69
   Lemon Garlic Shrimp Skewers with Quinoa 70
   Chicken and Vegetable Brown Rice Bowl 71
   Cabbage and White Bean Stew 72
   Vegetarian Stuffed Bell Peppers with Lentils 73
   Turkey and Quinoa Stuffed Acorn Squash 74
   Shrimp and Broccoli Alfredo with Whole Wheat Pasta 75
   Grilled Eggplant and Mozzarella Sandwich on Whole Grain Bread 76
   Asian-Inspired Beef and Broccoli Stir-Fry with Cauliflower Rice 77
   Chickpea Salad with Cucumber, Tomatoes, and Feta Cheese 78
   Lemon Dill Salmon Patties with Steamed Green Beans 79
   Vegetarian Lentil and Spinach Curry with Basmati Rice 80
   Turkey and Vegetable Lettuce Wraps with Hummus 81

DINNER 82

   Baked Tilapia with Herbed Quinoa and Steamed Asparagus 83
   Vegetarian Spinach and Chickpea Coconut Curry 84
   Turkey and Vegetable Kabobs with Brown Rice 85
   Lemon Herb Chicken Thighs with Cauliflower Mash 86
   Salmon and Zucchini Noodle Stir-Fry 87
   Spaghetti Squash with Tomato and Basil Sauce 88
   Miso-Glazed Cod with Stir-Fried Bok Choy 89
   Vegetarian Stuffed Portobello Mushrooms with Quinoa 90
   Grilled Shrimp Salad with Avocado and Mango 91

Chicken and Vegetable Korma with Basmati Rice 92
ZESTY LIME AND CILANTRO CHICKEN WITH CABBAGE SLAW 93
Egg Drop Soup with Shrimp and Vegetables 94
Mushroom and Spinach-Stuffed Chicken Breast with Green Beans 95
Quinoa and Black Bean Chili with Ground Turkey 96
Lemon Garlic Shrimp with Broccoli and Brown Rice 97
Stuffed Bell Peppers with Ground Chicken and Brown Rice 98
Chickpea and Tomato Curry with Cauliflower Rice 99
Sesame Ginger Beef Stir-Fry with Quinoa 100
Grilled Swordfish with Cucumber and Tomato Salad 101
Vegetarian Lentil and Sweet Potato Stew 102
Cilantro Lime Turkey Burger with Baked Sweet Potato Wedges 103
Caprese Zucchini Noodles with Grilled Chicken 104
Teriyaki Salmon with Quinoa and Steamed Spinach 105
Chicken and Vegetable Skillet with Quinoa 106
Roasted Red Pepper and Lentil Soup with Whole Wheat Bread 107
Mediterranean Stuffed Acorn Squash with Ground Turkey 108
Greek Lemon Chicken with Roasted Vegetables 109
Quinoa and Chickpea Stuffed Eggplant 110
Shrimp and Asparagus Risotto with Parmesan 111
Cabbage and White Bean Stir-Fry with Tofu 112

SMOOTHIES 113

Berry Blast Smoothie 114
Peachy Green Smoothie 115
Cucumber Mint Cooler 116
Cherry Almond Delight 117
Citrus Berry Fusion 118
Vanilla Date Smoothie 119
Apple Cinnamon Spice Smoothie 120
Mango Avocado Dream Smoothie 121
Pineapple Ginger Zing Smoothie 122
Blueberry Basil Bliss 123

CONCLUSION 124

Introduction

Living with significant organ failure is a challenging experience. Daily activities and dietary choices must be adjusted, as negligence can lead to adverse outcomes. Every action requires careful consideration and execution. Acquiring comprehensive knowledge about suitable foods, dietary restrictions, and the rationale behind avoiding specific foods is crucial for maintaining a consistent and closely monitored lifestyle.

This text provides insights into various renal illnesses, offering specifics on renal diets later on. It covers essential information such as what to eat, what to avoid, and guidelines for a more satisfying and stress-free life. The importance of meal planning and convenient meal preparation is thoroughly addressed. Additionally, dietary information is presented with suggestions for customization.

If you have been diagnosed with chronic kidney disease or any other kidney-related condition, it's essential to recognize that many individuals worldwide lead healthy lives despite facing similar health challenges. A diagnosis does not signify the end, and with proper care and lifestyle adjustments, you can continue to live a fulfilling and happy life. Adopting an appropriate eating plan can alleviate the strain on your kidneys and contribute to an overall healthier life, regardless of when the diagnosis occurred.

Taking care of yourself also involves considering the well-being of your loved ones. Your life is valued by those around you, and continuous improvement should be a goal. If implementing these changes seems daunting, don't hesitate to seek assistance from a loved one. This book serves as a guide through most aspects of the renal diet, but for specific health concerns, consulting a healthcare professional is always advisable.

Diet for the Kidneys

A renal diet emphasizes eating foods that will help to maintain the health of the kidneys. Reducing the progression and complications of renal illness, such as electrolyte imbalance, anemia, heart disease, etc., is advised for everyone with the condition. It involves limitations on the intake of fluids and on the amount of proteins, salt, potassium, phosphorus, and other minerals. Red meat, grains, fruits, and vegetables may need to be consumed in moderation.

The kind of protein they ought to consume is quite significant. Different people suffer from different kinds of renal disorders, and dietary adjustments are necessary based on the individual's condition. While some people just need to cut back on salt, others need to pay closer attention to how much potassium they consume. In order to get the most out of the diet, it might be necessary to talk about this with a physician or a trained dietitian.

Renal Diet Micronutrients

A person with renal illness has to keep an eye on a lot of nutrients. Among them are:

Sodium

Sodium is a crucial micronutrient that the body needs for many different kinds of processes, including controlling blood pressure, electrolyte balance, fluid volume, nerve impulses, and more. Because salt includes a lot of sodium, it is best to avoid consuming too much of it if you have renal disease. If the kidneys are unable to eliminate too much sodium, then it might cause serious damage. Heart disease, hypertension, and significant swelling in the lower leg and other regions of the body are possible complications. Additionally, it makes people thirstier, which puts more fluid on their compromised kidneys.

One way to cut back on salt is to eat less processed food, which typically contains more salt; consume fresh produce and meat that hasn't been preserved; check the labels on packaging to see how much salt is in it; and limit salt intake to 140 mg.

Calcium

This nutrient is also crucial for the heart's proper operation. It's present in a lot of foods. It is also necessary for the proper operation of muscles. When renal function is compromised, potassium levels rise; this condition is known as hyperkalemia. Numerous heart issues, including arrhythmias, muscular degeneration, cardiac attacks, and paralysis, may result from this. One can reduce their consumption of potassium by:

- Checking the potassium levels on packing labels.
- Eating fresh fruits and vegetables
- Steering clear of items high in potassium
- Monitoring the amount of potassium you eat each day

Phosphorus

For the body to operate properly, this vitamin is also crucial. It is necessary for the growth of some organs, connective tissues, and bones. The body will collect phosphorus if the kidneys are not functioning properly. Phosphorus causes the blood to have dangerously high levels of calcium and weakens bones by releasing calcium from them into the bloodstream. You may monitor your phosphorus intake by doing the following:

- Check the labels on packaged goods for PHOS levels.
- Steer clear of meals that are high in phosphorus.

Consuming meat that is of superior quality and low in fat.

Fresh fruits and veggies

Proteins

A condition known as high blood protein and amino acid levels arises when the kidneys are unable to adequately remove excess protein from the body. Numerous issues arise as a result of the broken-down proteins and their waste products circulating throughout the body. Additionally, it harms the kidneys' structural integrity. It might be difficult to determine how much protein an individual needs to eat because it depends on their own health. In general, eating high-quality protein and consuming less red meat are stressful. A physician or dietician should be consulted for comprehensive advice.

Water Consumption

In severe situations, dialysis is required to help filter out the extra water in the body due to improper kidney function. The individual should consume the least quantity of liquids feasible to lessen the strain on their kidneys. By placing additional strain on other organs like the heart and lungs, excess fluid can harm them. You can monitor how much fluid you consume by doing the following:

- Steer clear of hot and salty foods;

- Take medication with sips of water;

- Record how much fluid you consume with your meals in a journal;

- Steer clear of salty condiments, such as soy sauce.

- Consuming cold beverages;

- Adhering to medical professionals' advice on what to and shouldn't be consumed.

Foods for Renal Diet

You should routinely check the foods you eat on a daily basis. You should consume less salt, potassium, and phosphorus in order to promote general wellness. You also need to consume less fluid overall and eat more high-quality protein. This comprehensive list of things to eat and things to avoid will help you choose your next meal more easily.

Items High in Sodium That You Should Steer Clear of:

- Various meats and sausages. Pork, chicken, and cuts that have been cured, smoked, or preserved.
- Preserved fish and seafood
- Dinners that are packed or frozen
- Food items that are canned, such as soup or pasta
- Salted nuts
- Roasted and canned beans
- Buttermilk
- Cheese, cheese products, processed cottage cheese
- Extra-salted bread and quick bread
- Salted rolls
- Biscuits and pancakes produced with self-rising flour or its mixtures
- Salted crackers
- The dough of pasta, potatoes, and rice that is processed and packaged
- Vegetables and vegetable juices in cans
- Salted regular pickles, as well as olives and other pickled vegetables.
- Vegetables made with pork products
- The dough of hash browns and scalloped potatoes, which are processed and packaged.
- Quick pasta meals
- Processed ketchup
- Processed and salted mustard
- Processed salsa
- Dehydrated or regular soups can
- Processed or regular broths
- Cup noodles processed and salted ramen mixes
- Soya sauce
- Seasoning salts

- Marinades which are salted
- Salad dressings in bottles, processed or regular
- Salad dressings with bacon
- Salted butter and margarine
- Instant custard or pudding
- Ready to eat cakes

Foods Low in Sodium That Are Better to Eat:

- Pork, lamb, chicken, beef, fish, shrimp, and poultry pieces, both fresh and frozen.
- Water- and oil-packed, drained fish and poultry; low-sodium canned fish;
- Eggs and egg substitutes;
- Dried peas rather than canned beans;
- Low-sodium plant-based yogurts, almond, rice, or coconut milk
- Low-sodium cheeses such as ricotta and parmesan, as well as low-sodium cream cheese
- Ready-to-eat cereals
- Unsalted bread and rolls
- Whole-wheat, almond, coconut, low-sodium plain, and all-purpose white flour
- Low-sodium corn and tortillas
- Low-sodium crackers, popcorn without salt, chips, and breadsticks
- Low-sodium noodles, unsalted pasta, and grains
- Fresh or frozen veggies, low-sodium canned veggies without sauce or seasoning
- Low-sodium vegetable juices, V-8, and low-sodium tomato juice
- Low-sodium pickles
- Fresh potatoes or unsalted and unseasoned frozen french fries and mashed potatoes
- Fresh and frozen canned fruits, dried fruits
- Low-sodium salsa
- Low-sodium soups that are canned
- Homemade broths made without salt and fresh ingredients
- Homemade pasta without salt
- Low-sodium soy sauce
- Low-sodium salad dressings
- Low-sodium mayonnaise
- Unsalted butter and margarine, vegetable oils
- Homemade ketchup that is unsalted
- Foods high in potassium that you should stay away from include fried onions, sweet potatoes, broccoli, beets, okra, and cooked spinach.
- Bananas, avocados, mango, orange, pomegranate, prune, pumpkin, coconut, cantaloupe, honeydew, and bananas
- Shakes and buttermilk
- Beans, either roasted or refried; legumes such as lentils; nuts such as

walnuts and raisins; granola; whole grains and bran; fast foods such as french fries and other salty foods; processed meats; vegetable juices; tomato sauce; and fruit juices like pomegranate and prune juice.

- Soups and creams
- Regular and frozen yogurt
- Ice creams
- Sweet dishes with chocolate

Foods Low in Potassium That You Must Consume in Their Place:

- Apples, grapes, pineapple, peaches, plum, all berries, watermelon
- Rice milk
- Green beans and snow peas
- Dried cranberries
- Unsalted popcorn
- Hash browns and mash potatoes composed of leached potatoes
- Low sodium tomato and V-8 juice
- Unsalted sauces and apple sauce
- Unsalted noodles and pasta
- Non-dairy creams
- Sherbet with flavors of lemon and vanilla instead of chocolate

Foods High in Phosphorus That Should Be Avoided:

- Certain fruits
- Certain vegetables
- Parts of chicken and other fowl
- Ham and other pork products
- Hunted animals
- Some seafood
- Plain bread
- Tortillas
- Muffin
- Some pasta
- Some varieties of rice
- Certain cheeses
- Milk
- Yogurt
- Ice cream
- Eggs
- Snacks

Foods Low in Phosphorus That Are Better to Eat:

- Carrots, radishes, and baby carrots

- Apples, cherries, peaches, pineapples, blueberries, and strawberries

- Pot roast beef, sirloin steak

- Skinless chicken and turkey, breast and thighs

- Porkchop, mostly lean pork patty and pork roast

- Veal chop

- Wild salmon, mahi mahi, king crab, lobster, snow crab, oyster shrimp, water, or oil-packed canned tuna.

- Plain bread without salt, Italian bread, blueberry bread, sourdough bread, white bread, flatbread, wheat bread, pita bread, and cinnamon bread

- Flour tortillas, corn tortillas

- English muffins

- Cream cheese, parmesan, blue cheese, feta, and couscous; long-grain white rice

- Rice, soy, and almond milk

- Salted popcorn, pasteurized egg whites, sorbet, and non-dairy creamer

Protein Options That Are Beneficial to the Kidneys That Are Included in the Whole Diet:

- Skinless chicken breast and thighs

- Fish and shrimp (salmon, trout, mackerel, and shrimp)

- Pork chops

- Cottage cheese

- Pasteurized egg

- Greek yogurt

- Shakes made with rice, almond, coconut, or soy milk

Kidney-friendly beverage alternatives that are part of this diet include:

- Fruits like apples, cherries, grapes, berries, peaches, and plums

- Vegetables such as bell peppers, carrots, celery, lettuce, and eggplant

- Tea and coffee, ice cubes, gelatin, fruit juices, popsicles, milk substitute, sherbet, and low-sodium soups

Meal plan

Sticking to a nutrition plan is crucial when following a kidney diet, as it plays a pivotal role in managing kidney health and preventing complications associated with kidney disease. Adhering to a well-designed nutrition plan can help individuals with kidney issues maintain better overall health, slow down the progression of kidney disease, and improve their quality of life. Here are some key reasons why it's essential to stick to a kidney-friendly nutrition plan:

Manage Nutrient Intake: A kidney diet is carefully crafted to regulate the intake of nutrients such as sodium, potassium, phosphorus, and protein. These adjustments are necessary to prevent the accumulation of waste products in the blood, maintain fluid balance, and alleviate the burden on the kidneys.

Control Blood Pressure: High blood pressure is a common complication of kidney disease. Following a kidney-friendly nutrition plan, which typically includes reducing sodium intake, can help manage blood pressure levels and reduce the strain on the kidneys.

Balance Electrolytes: Potassium and phosphorus are electrolytes that need to be carefully regulated in a kidney diet. High levels of these minerals can lead to complications, such as electrolyte imbalances and bone issues. Adhering to a nutrition plan helps strike the right balance.

Prevent Fluid Retention: Kidneys play a crucial role in regulating fluid balance. A kidney diet often includes monitoring fluid intake to prevent fluid retention, which can lead to swelling and other complications.

Advice for Sticking to a Kidney Diet:

Consult a Dietitian: Seek guidance from a registered dietitian who specializes in kidney health. They can create a personalized nutrition plan tailored to your specific needs, taking into account your health status, preferences, and lifestyle.

Educate yourself: Understanding the principles of a kidney-friendly diet empowers you to make informed food choices. Learn to read food labels and identify high- and low-potassium, low-phosphorus, and low-sodium options.

Meal Planning: Plan your meals and snacks in advance to ensure that you meet your nutritional goals. This can help you avoid impulsive food choices that may not align with your kidney diet.

Stay Hydrated: While fluid intake may be restricted, it's essential to stay adequately hydrated. Work with your healthcare team to determine the appropriate amount of fluids for your specific needs.

Monitor Lab Results: Regularly monitor your lab results, including blood tests, to assess how well you are managing your kidney health through your nutrition plan. Adjustments can be made based on these results.

Communicate with the healthcare team: Keep an open line of communication with your healthcare team. Report any changes in your health status, and work together to make necessary adjustments to your nutrition plan.

Remember, adherence to a kidney diet is a long-term commitment that requires dedication and support. By following your nutrition plan diligently, you can actively participate in managing your kidney health and improving your overall well-being.

Healthy Weekly Meal Plan

DAY	BREAKFAST	LUNCH	DINNER
monday	Oatmeal with Sliced Bananas and Almonds	Tuna Salad Lettuce Wraps with Cherry Tomatoes	Baked Tilapia with Herbed Quinoa and Steamed Asparagus
tuesday	Scrambled Eggs with Spinach and Feta Cheese	Eggplant and Zucchini Lasagna with Ground Turkey	Vegetarian Spinach and Chickpea Coconut Curry
wednesday	Whole Grain Toast with Avocado Slices and Cherry Tomatoes	Salmon and Asparagus Foil Packets with Lemon	Turkey and Vegetable Kabobs with Brown Rice
thursday	Cottage Cheese Parfait with Pineapple and Walnuts	Mediterranean Chickpea and Vegetable Bowl	Lemon Herb Chicken Thighs with Cauliflower Mash
friday	Brown Rice Cake with Cream Cheese and Smoked Salmon	Turkey and Vegetable Stir-Fry with Quinoa	Salmon and Zucchini Noodle Stir-Fry
saturday	Quinoa Breakfast Bowl with Berries and Almond Milk	Roasted Vegetable and Lentil Soup	Miso-Glazed Cod with Stir-Fried Bok Choy
sunday	Greek Yogurt Pancakes with Blueberries	Caprese Chicken Skewers with Basil Pesto	Grilled Shrimp Salad with Avocado and Mango

Healthy Weekly Meal Plan

DAY	BREAKFAST	LUNCH	DINNER
monday	Whole Grain Toast with Avocado Slices and Cherry Tomatoes	Quinoa and Black-Eyed Pea Salad with Herbs	Chicken and Vegetable Korma with Basmati Rice
tuesday	Poached Eggs over Sauteed Spinach and Mushrooms	Zoodle (Zucchini Noodle) Primavera with Grilled Chicken	Zesty Lime and Cilantro Chicken with Cabbage Slaw
wednesday	Vegetable Omelette with Herbs	Low-Sodium Minestrone Soup with Whole Wheat Bread	Egg Drop Soup with Shrimp and Vegetables
thursday	Buckwheat Pancakes with Strawberries	Baked Sweet Potato with Kidney Beans and Salsa	Quinoa and Black Bean Chili with Ground Turkey
friday	Cantaloupe and Honeydew Melon Salad	Sesame Ginger Tofu Stir-Fry with Brown Rice	Lemon Garlic Shrimp with Broccoli and Brown Rice
saturday	Sweet Potato Hash with Poached Eggs	Lemon Garlic Shrimp Skewers with Quinoa	Chickpea and Tomato Curry with Cauliflower Rice
sunday	Steamed Asparagus with Soft-Boiled Eggs	Cabbage and White Bean Stew	Sesame Ginger Beef Stir-Fry with Quinoa

Healthy Weekly Meal Plan

DAY	BREAKFAST	LUNCH	DINNER
monday	Low-Phosphorus Bran Muffins with Apple Compote	Lemon Garlic Shrimp Skewers with Quinoa	Vegetarian Lentil and Sweet Potato Stew
tuesday	Brown Rice Porridge with Cinnamon and Raisins	Chicken and Vegetable Brown Rice Bowl	Grilled Swordfish with Cucumber and Tomato Salad
wednesday	Cherry Almond Breakfast Quinoa	Shrimp and Broccoli Alfredo with Whole Wheat Pasta	Cilantro Lime Turkey Burger with Baked Sweet Potato Wedges
thursday	Spinach and Mushroom Breakfast Quesadilla	Asian-Inspired Beef and Broccoli Stir-Fry with Cauliflower Rice	Caprese Zucchini Noodles with Grilled Chicken
friday	Cauliflower Hash Browns with Poached Eggs	Lemon Dill Salmon Patties with Steamed Green Beans	Teriyaki Salmon with Quinoa and Steamed Spinach
saturday	Papaya Boat with Cottage Cheese and Lime	Vegetarian Lentil and Spinach Curry with Basmati Rice	Chicken and Vegetable Skillet with Quinoa
sunday	Quinoa Breakfast Bowl with Berries and Almond Milk	Turkey and Vegetable Lettuce Wraps with Hummus	Quinoa and Chickpea Stuffed Eggplant

Healthy Weekly Meal Plan

DAY	BREAKFAST	LUNCH	DINNER
monday	Vegetable Omelette with Herbs	Quinoa and Black-Eyed Pea Salad with Herbs	Cabbage and White Bean Stir-Fry with Tofu
tuesday	Chia Seed Pudding with Mango and Coconut Flakes	Caprese Chicken Skewers with Basil Pesto	Chickpea and Tomato Curry with Cauliflower Rice
wednesday	Greek Yogurt Pancakes with Blueberries	Roasted Vegetable and Lentil Soup	Lemon Garlic Shrimp with Broccoli and Brown Rice
thursday	Cottage Cheese Parfait with Pineapple and Walnuts	Turkey and Vegetable Stir-Fry with Quinoa	Zesty Lime and Cilantro Chicken with Cabbage Slaw
friday	Cherry Almond Breakfast Quinoa	Salmon and Asparagus Foil Packets with Lemon	Grilled Shrimp Salad with Avocado and Mango
saturday	Spinach and Mushroom Breakfast Quesadilla	Tuna Salad Lettuce Wraps with Cherry Tomatoes	Chicken and Vegetable Korma with Basmati Rice
sunday	Oatmeal with Sliced Bananas and Almonds	Baked Sweet Potato with Kidney Beans and Salsa	Salmon and Zucchini Noodle Stir-Fry

Breakfast

Oatmeal with Sliced Bananas and Almonds

2 servings | 10 minutes

Cal 188
Fat 8 g
Carb 48 g
Protein 8 g

Sodium 80 mg
Potassium 400 mg
Phosphorus 150 mg

INGREDIENTS
- 1 cup old-fashioned oats
- 2 cups water
- 1/2 cup unsweetened almond milk
- 1 banana, sliced
- 2 tablespoons sliced almonds
- 1 teaspoon ground cinnamon
- 1 tablespoon honey (optional, for sweetness)

DIRECTIONS
1. In a medium-sized saucepan, bring 2 cups of water to a boil.
2. Add the old-fashioned oats to the boiling water, reduce heat to low, and let it simmer for 5-7 minutes, stirring occasionally.
3. Once the oats have absorbed most of the water and have a creamy consistency, add the almond milk and continue to cook for an additional 2-3 minutes.
4. Remove the saucepan from the heat. Stir in the ground cinnamon.
5. Divide the oatmeal into two serving bowls.
6. Top each bowl with sliced bananas and sliced almonds.
7. Drizzle honey over the oatmeal if additional sweetness is desired.
8. Allow the oatmeal to cool for a minute before serving.

Scrambled Eggs with Spinach and Feta Cheese

2 servings | 10 minutes

Cal 320
Fat 15 g
Carb 3 g
Protein 18 g

Sodium 300 mg
Potassium 350 mg
Phosphorus 250 mg

INGREDIENTS

- 4 large eggs
- 1 cup fresh spinach, chopped
- 1/4 cup crumbled feta cheese
- 2 teaspoons olive oil
- Salt and pepper to taste
- Fresh herbs (optional, for garnish)

DIRECTIONS

1. Crack the eggs into a bowl and whisk them together until well combined. Season with salt and pepper.
2. Heat olive oil in a non-stick skillet over medium heat.
3. Add chopped spinach to the skillet and sauté for 1-2 minutes until wilted.
4. Pour the whisked eggs over the spinach in the skillet.
5. Gently stir the eggs and spinach together with a spatula, ensuring even cooking.
6. As the eggs begin to set, add crumbled feta cheese to the mixture.
7. Continue to cook, stirring occasionally, until the eggs are fully cooked but still moist.
8. Remove the skillet from heat.
9. Garnish with fresh herbs if desired.
10. Serve the scrambled eggs with spinach and feta on a plate.

Smoothie (Berries, Apple, Greek Yogurt, and Ice)

2 servings | 5 minutes

Cal 150
Fat 2 g
Carb 28 g
Protein 10 g

Sodium 30 mg
Potassium 200 mg
Phosphorus 100 mg

INGREDIENTS

- 1/2 cup mixed berries (such as blueberries, strawberries, and raspberries)
- 1 small apple, peeled, cored, and chopped
- 1/2 cup plain Greek yogurt (low-phosphorus)
- 1 cup ice cubes
- 1/2 cup water or almond milk (unsweetened)

Optional Add-ins:
- 1 tablespoon chia seeds (for extra fiber)
- 1 teaspoon honey (for sweetness, optional)

DIRECTIONS

1. Place the mixed berries, chopped apple, Greek yogurt, ice cubes, and water (or almond milk) in a blender.
2. Blend on high speed until the mixture reaches a smooth consistency.
3. If the smoothie is too thick, you can add more water or almond milk in small amounts until you achieve your desired consistency.
4. Taste the smoothie and adjust sweetness if necessary by adding honey (optional).
5. Pour the smoothie into a glass and enjoy immediately.

Whole Grain Toast with Avocado Slices and Cherry Tomatoes

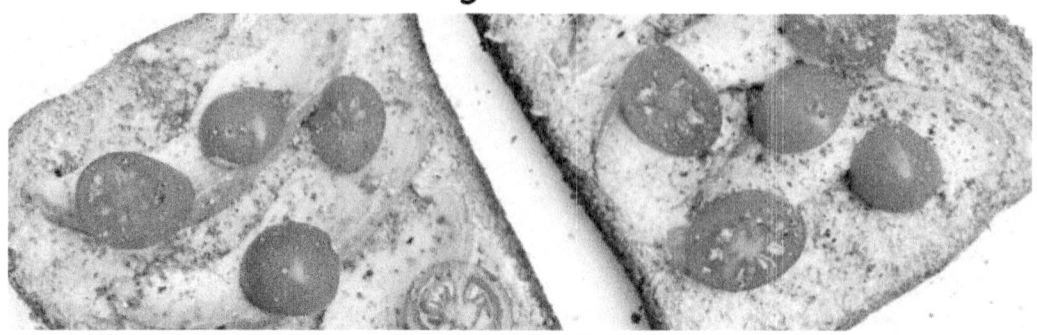

2 servings | 15 minutes

Cal 280
Fat 16 g
Carb 32 g
Protein 5 g

Sodium 150 mg
Potassium 450 mg
Phosphorus 120 mg

INGREDIENTS

- 2 slices of whole grain bread (low-sodium, if available)
- 1 ripe avocado, sliced
- 1 cup cherry tomatoes, halved
- 1 tablespoon extra-virgin olive oil
- Salt and pepper to taste
- Fresh cilantro or basil for garnish (optional)

DIRECTIONS

1. Toast the whole grain bread slices to your desired level of crispiness.
2. While the bread is toasting, slice the avocado and halve the cherry tomatoes.
3. Once the toast is ready, drizzle each slice with extra-virgin olive oil.
4. Layer the sliced avocado evenly on top of the toast.
5. Scatter the halved cherry tomatoes over the avocado.
6. Season with salt and pepper to taste.
7. Garnish with fresh cilantro or basil if desired.
8. Serve immediately.

Cottage Cheese Parfait with Pineapple and Walnuts

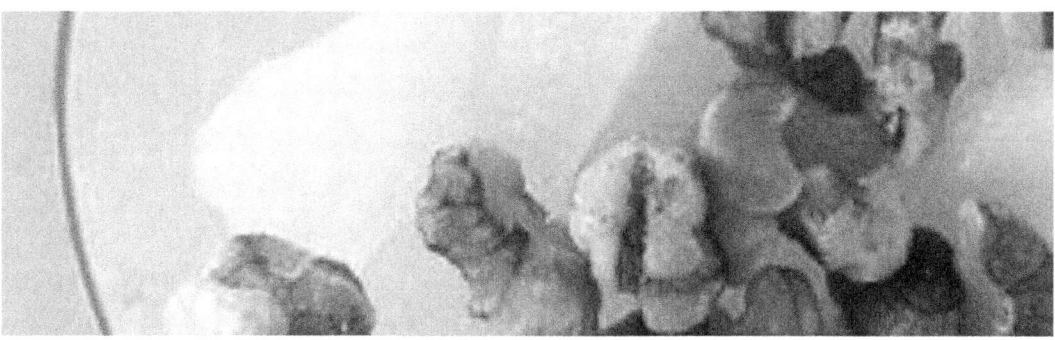

2 servings | 15 minutes

Cal 280
Fat 10 g
Carb 20 g
Protein 26 g

Sodium 300 mg
Potassium 380 mg
Phosphorus 230 mg

INGREDIENTS

- 1 cup low-fat cottage cheese
- 1 cup fresh pineapple chunks
- 2 tablespoons chopped walnuts
- 1 teaspoon honey (optional, for drizzling)
- 1/2 teaspoon vanilla extract
- Fresh mint leaves for garnish (optional)

DIRECTIONS

1. In a bowl, mix the cottage cheese with vanilla extract until well combined.
2. In serving glasses or bowls, layer the cottage cheese with fresh pineapple chunks.
3. Sprinkle chopped walnuts over each layer.
4. Repeat the layers until you reach the top of the glass or bowl.
5. If desired, drizzle honey on top for a touch of sweetness.
6. Garnish with fresh mint leaves for a burst of freshness (optional).
7. Serve immediately and enjoy.

Brown Rice Cake with Cream Cheese and Smoked Salmon

2 servings | 5 minutes

Cal 220
Fat 8 g
Carb 28 g
Protein 12 g

Sodium 450 mg
Potassium 180 mg
Phosphorus 200 mg

INGREDIENTS

- 2 brown rice cakes
- 2 tablespoons low-fat cream cheese
- 2 ounces smoked salmon
- 1 tablespoon fresh dill, chopped
- 1 teaspoon capers (optional)
- Lemon wedges for serving

DIRECTIONS

1. Spread a tablespoon of low-fat cream cheese evenly on each brown rice cake.
2. Place smoked salmon slices on top of the cream cheese.
3. Sprinkle chopped fresh dill over the smoked salmon.
4. Optionally, add capers for a burst of flavor.
5. Serve with lemon wedges on the side for squeezing over the top.
6. Enjoy this delicious and kidney-friendly open-faced sandwich.

Quinoa Breakfast Bowl with Berries and Almond Milk

2 servings | 25 minutes

Cal 300
Fat 8 g
Carb 47 g
Protein 9 g

Sodium 100 mg
Potassium 280 mg
Phosphorus 180 mg

INGREDIENTS

- 1/2 cup quinoa, rinsed
- 1 cup unsweetened almond milk
- 1/2 cup mixed berries (blueberries, strawberries, raspberries)
- 1 tablespoon sliced almonds
- 1 teaspoon chia seeds
- 1 teaspoon honey (optional, for drizzling)
- 1/2 teaspoon vanilla extract

DIRECTIONS

1. In a small saucepan, combine the rinsed quinoa and almond milk. Bring to a boil.
2. Reduce heat to low, cover, and simmer for 15 minutes or until quinoa is cooked and the liquid is absorbed.
3. Stir in the vanilla extract during the last few minutes of cooking.
4. Remove from heat and let it sit, covered, for 5 minutes. Fluff with a fork.
5. Transfer the cooked quinoa to a bowl.
6. Top the quinoa with mixed berries, sliced almonds, and chia seeds.
7. Drizzle honey over the top for added sweetness if desired.
8. Mix gently to combine the ingredients.
9. Serve warm and enjoy your nutritious quinoa breakfast bowl.

Poached Eggs over Sautéed Spinach and Mushrooms

2 servings | 15 minutes

Cal 240
Fat 18 g
Carb 7 g
Protein 14 g
Sodium 150 mg
Potassium 650 mg
Phosphorus 200 mg

INGREDIENTS

- 2 large eggs
- 2 cups fresh spinach, washed and chopped
- 1 cup mushrooms, sliced
- 1 tablespoon olive oil
- Salt and pepper to taste
- 1 teaspoon white vinegar (for poaching)
- Parmesan cheese for garnish (optional)
- Fresh herbs (such as parsley or chives) for garnish

DIRECTIONS

1. In a skillet, heat olive oil over medium heat.
2. Add sliced mushrooms to the skillet and sauté until they release their moisture and become golden brown.
3. Add chopped spinach to the skillet and sauté until wilted. Season with salt and pepper to taste.
4. Meanwhile, fill a shallow pan with water and bring it to a gentle simmer. Add white vinegar to the simmering water.
5. Crack each egg into a small bowl. Create a gentle whirlpool in the simmering water and carefully slide the eggs into the water one at a time. Poach for about 3-4 minutes for a runny yolk or longer if you prefer a firmer yolk.
6. While the eggs are poaching, arrange the sautéed spinach and mushrooms on a plate.
7. Using a slotted spoon, carefully lift each poached egg out of the water and place it on top of the spinach and mushrooms.
8. Garnish with Parmesan cheese and fresh herbs if desired.

Homemade Muesli with Low-Potassium Fruit

2 servings | 5 minutes

Cal 350
Fat 12 g
Carb 50 g
Protein 10 g

Sodium 70 mg
Potassium 300 mg
Phosphorus 150 mg

INGREDIENTS

- 1 cup rolled oats
- 2 tablespoons chia seeds
- 1/4 cup unsalted sunflower seeds
- 1/4 cup chopped almonds
- 1/4 cup dried cranberries (unsweetened)
- 1 teaspoon ground cinnamon
- 1 cup low-potassium fruit (e.g., apples, pears), diced
- 1 cup low-fat milk or a dairy-free alternative

DIRECTIONS

1. In a large mixing bowl, combine rolled oats, chia seeds, sunflower seeds, chopped almonds, dried cranberries, and ground cinnamon.
2. Mix the ingredients thoroughly to ensure an even distribution.
3. Add the diced low-potassium fruit (e.g., apples, pears) to the mixture and stir gently.
4. Divide the muesli into two serving bowls.
5. Pour half a cup of low-fat milk or a dairy-free alternative over each serving.
6. Allow the muesli to soak for a few minutes, or refrigerate overnight for a convenient grab-and-go breakfast.
7. Before serving, you can add a little more milk to adjust the consistency to your liking.

Greek Yogurt Pancakes with Blueberries

2 servings | 20 minutes

Cal 300
Fat 5 g
Carb 50 g
Protein 15 g

Sodium 350 mg
Potassium 280 mg
Phosphorus 200 mg

INGREDIENTS

- 1 cup whole wheat flour
- 1 teaspoon baking powder
- 1/2 teaspoon baking soda
- 1/4 teaspoon salt
- 1 cup Greek yogurt (low-fat)
- 1/2 cup unsweetened almond milk (or any low-potassium milk)
- 1 large egg
- 1 tablespoon honey (optional)
- 1 cup fresh blueberries
- Cooking spray or a small amount of oil for the pan

DIRECTIONS

1. In a mixing bowl, whisk together the whole wheat flour, baking powder, baking soda, and salt.
2. In a separate bowl, combine Greek yogurt, almond milk, egg, and honey (if using).
3. Add the wet ingredients to the dry ingredients, stirring until just combined. Be careful not to overmix; a few lumps are okay.
4. Gently fold in the fresh blueberries.
5. Preheat a non-stick skillet or griddle over medium heat and lightly coat with cooking spray or a small amount of oil.
6. Pour 1/4 cup portions of batter onto the skillet for each pancake.
7. Cook until bubbles form on the surface of the pancake, then flip and cook the other side until golden brown.
8. Continue with the remaining batter.
9. Serve the Greek yogurt pancakes warm, topped with additional blueberries if desired.

Chia Seed Pudding with Mango and Coconut Flakes

2 servings | 4 hours

Cal 250
Fat 13 g
Carb 50 g
Protein 6 g

Sodium 80 mg
Potassium 220 mg
Phosphorus 150 mg

INGREDIENTS

- 1/4 cup chia seeds
- 1 cup unsweetened almond milk (or any low-potassium milk)
- 1 tablespoon honey or maple syrup (optional, for sweetness)
- 1/2 teaspoon vanilla extract
- 1 ripe mango, peeled and diced
- 2 tablespoons unsweetened coconut flakes

DIRECTIONS

1. In a bowl, combine chia seeds, almond milk, honey (or maple syrup), and vanilla extract. Stir well to ensure the chia seeds are evenly distributed.
2. Cover the bowl and refrigerate for at least 4 hours or overnight, allowing the chia seeds to absorb the liquid and form a pudding-like consistency.
3. Stir the chia seed pudding before serving to ensure an even texture.
4. In serving glasses or bowls, layer the chia seed pudding with diced mango.
5. Top each serving with unsweetened coconut flakes.
6. Drizzle additional honey or maple syrup on top if you prefer extra sweetness.

Vegetable Omelette with Herbs

2 servings | 10 minutes

Cal 250
Fat 18 g
Carb 5 g
Protein 16 g
Sodium 220 mg
Potassium 350 mg
Phosphorus 280 mg

INGREDIENTS

- 3 large eggs
- 1/4 cup bell peppers, diced
- 1/4 cup tomatoes, diced
- 1/4 cup spinach, chopped
- 1/4 cup mushrooms, sliced
- 1 tablespoon olive oil
- 1 tablespoon fresh herbs (such as parsley, chives, or cilantro), chopped
- Salt and pepper to taste
- Optional: 2 tablespoons feta cheese (low-phosphorus), crumbled

DIRECTIONS

1. In a bowl, whisk the eggs until well beaten. Season with salt and pepper.
2. Heat olive oil in a non-stick skillet over medium heat.
3. Add bell peppers, tomatoes, spinach, and mushrooms to the skillet. Sauté until vegetables are softened.
4. Pour the beaten eggs evenly over the sautéed vegetables.
5. Allow the eggs to set slightly at the edges. Gently lift the edges with a spatula, tilting the skillet to let the uncooked eggs flow underneath.
6. When the omelette is mostly set but still slightly runny on top, sprinkle fresh herbs (and optional feta cheese) over one half.
7. Carefully fold the other half of the omelette over the herbs and cheese.
8. Cook for an additional 1-2 minutes until the cheese melts and the omelette is cooked through.
9. Slide the vegetable omelette onto a plate.
10. Garnish with additional herbs if desired.

Low-Sodium Veggies and Egg White Scramble

2 servings | 10 minutes

Cal 150
Fat 8 g
Carb 8 g
Protein 15 g

Sodium 150 mg
Potassium 400 mg
Phosphorus 120 mg

INGREDIENTS

- 1 cup mixed vegetables (such as bell peppers, tomatoes, spinach, mushrooms), chopped
- 4 large egg whites
- 1 tablespoon olive oil
- 1/4 teaspoon garlic powder
- Salt and pepper to taste
- Fresh herbs (such as parsley or chives) for garnish

DIRECTIONS

1. Heat olive oil in a non-stick skillet over medium heat.
2. Add the chopped vegetables to the skillet and sauté until they are tender.
3. In a bowl, whisk the egg whites until frothy.
4. Pour the whisked egg whites over the sautéed vegetables.
5. Sprinkle garlic powder, salt, and pepper over the eggs and vegetables.
6. Gently scramble the eggs and vegetables together until the eggs are fully cooked.
7. Remove the skillet from heat.
8. Garnish with fresh herbs.
9. Serve the low-sodium veggies and egg white scramble hot.

Buckwheat Pancakes with Strawberries

2 servings | 20 minutes

Cal 250
Fat 7 g
Carb 40 g
Protein 8 g
Sodium 320 mg
Potassium 280 mg
Phosphorus 150 mg

INGREDIENTS

- 1 cup buckwheat flour
- 1 tablespoon sugar (optional)
- 1 teaspoon baking powder
- 1/2 teaspoon baking soda
- 1/4 teaspoon salt
- 1 cup low-fat buttermilk
- 1 large egg
- 1 tablespoon unsalted butter, melted
- Fresh strawberries, sliced, for topping
- Maple syrup (optional, for drizzling)

DIRECTIONS

1. In a mixing bowl, combine buckwheat flour, sugar (if using), baking powder, baking soda, and salt.
2. In a separate bowl, whisk together buttermilk, egg, and melted butter.
3. Pour the wet ingredients into the dry ingredients and stir until just combined. Do not overmix; a few lumps are okay.
4. Preheat a non-stick skillet or griddle over medium heat.
5. Scoop 1/4 cup portions of batter onto the skillet for each pancake.
6. Cook until bubbles form on the surface of the pancake, then flip and cook the other side until golden brown.
7. Repeat with the remaining batter.
8. Serve the buckwheat pancakes topped with fresh strawberry slices.
9. Drizzle with maple syrup if desired.

Sweet Potato Hash with Poached Eggs

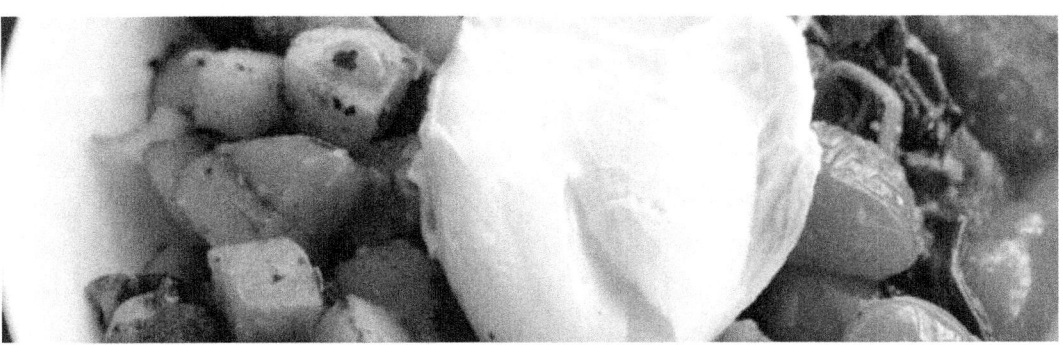

2 servings — 30 minutes

Cal 320
Fat 15 g
Carb 38 g
Protein 12 g
Sodium 160 mg
Potassium 800 mg
Phosphorus 180 mg

INGREDIENTS

- 2 medium sweet potatoes, peeled and diced
- 1 red bell pepper, diced
- 1 small onion, finely chopped
- 2 cloves garlic, minced
- 2 tablespoons olive oil
- 1 teaspoon smoked paprika
- 1/2 teaspoon cumin
- Salt and pepper to taste
- 4 large eggs
- Fresh parsley or chives for garnish (optional)
- Hot sauce or salsa for serving (optional)

DIRECTIONS

1. In a large skillet, heat olive oil over medium heat.
2. Add chopped sweet potatoes to the skillet and cook for 5-7 minutes, stirring occasionally, until they begin to soften.
3. Add diced red bell pepper, chopped onion, and minced garlic to the skillet. Continue to cook for an additional 5-7 minutes until vegetables are tender.
4. Sprinkle smoked paprika, cumin, salt, and pepper over the sweet potato hash. Stir to combine, allowing the spices to coat the vegetables.
5. Create four small wells in the hash with a spoon and crack one egg into each well.
6. Cover the skillet with a lid and poach the eggs for 5-7 minutes or until the egg whites are set, and the yolks are still slightly runny.
7. Once the eggs are poached to your liking, remove the skillet from heat.
8. Garnish with fresh parsley or chives if desired.
9. Serve the sweet potato hash with poached eggs hot, with optional hot sauce or salsa on the side.

Cantaloupe and Honeydew Melon Salad

2 servings | 40 minutes

Cal 80
Fat 1 g
Carb 18 g
Protein 2 g

Sodium 20 mg
Potassium 350 mg
Phosphorus 30 mg

INGREDIENTS

- 2 cups cantaloupe, peeled, seeded, and cubed
- 2 cups honeydew melon, peeled, seeded, and cubed
- 1 tablespoon fresh mint, chopped
- 1 tablespoon lime juice
- 1 teaspoon honey (optional)
- 1/4 cup slivered almonds, toasted (optional)

DIRECTIONS

1. In a large bowl, combine the cubed cantaloupe and honeydew melon.
2. In a small bowl, whisk together lime juice and honey (if using).
3. Pour the lime-honey dressing over the melon cubes and gently toss to coat.
4. Sprinkle chopped fresh mint over the melon mixture and toss again.
5. If desired, top the salad with toasted slivered almonds for added crunch and flavor.
6. Chill the salad in the refrigerator for at least 30 minutes before serving.
7. Serve the Cantaloupe and Honeydew Melon Salad in individual bowls or on a platter.

Homemade Granola with Low-Phosphorus Nuts

2 servings | 35 minutes

Cal 220
Fat 11 g
Carb 28 g
Protein 5 g
Sodium 40 mg
Potassium 120 mg
Phosphorus 85 mg

INGREDIENTS

- 2 cups old-fashioned oats
- 1/2 cup chopped almonds (low-phosphorus)
- 1/4 cup unsweetened coconut flakes
- 2 tablespoons chia seeds
- 1/4 cup honey or maple syrup
- 2 tablespoons coconut oil, melted
- 1 teaspoon vanilla extract
- 1/2 teaspoon cinnamon
- 1/4 teaspoon salt
- 1/2 cup raisins or dried cranberries (optional, choose lower phosphorus options)

DIRECTIONS

1. Preheat the oven to 325°F (163°C) and line a baking sheet with parchment paper.
2. In a large mixing bowl, combine oats, chopped almonds, coconut flakes, and chia seeds.
3. In a separate bowl, whisk together honey or maple syrup, melted coconut oil, vanilla extract, cinnamon, and salt.
4. Pour the wet mixture over the dry ingredients and stir until everything is well coated.
5. Spread the granola mixture evenly on the prepared baking sheet.
6. Bake for 20-25 minutes or until the granola is golden brown, stirring halfway through to ensure even cooking.
7. Remove from the oven and let it cool completely. The granola will become crisp as it cools.
8. If desired, add raisins or dried cranberries once the granola has cooled.
9. Store the homemade granola in an airtight container.

Steamed Asparagus with Soft-Boiled Eggs

2 servings | 15 minutes

Cal 200
Fat 14 g
Carb 7 g
Protein 14 g
Sodium 100 mg
Potassium 430 mg
Phosphorus 220 mg

INGREDIENTS

- 1 bunch of asparagus, tough ends trimmed
- 4 large eggs
- 1 tablespoon olive oil
- Salt and pepper to taste
- Lemon wedges for serving (optional)
- Fresh parsley for garnish (optional)

DIRECTIONS

1. In a steamer basket over boiling water, steam the asparagus for 3-5 minutes or until crisp-tender. Remove from heat.
2. While the asparagus is steaming, bring a small pot of water to a gentle boil.
3. Carefully add the eggs to the boiling water and cook for 6 minutes for a soft-boiled consistency.
4. Once the eggs are done, transfer them to a bowl of cold water to stop the cooking process. Peel the eggs and set them aside.
5. Drizzle olive oil over the steamed asparagus and season with salt and pepper.
6. Arrange the steamed asparagus on a serving plate.
7. Cut the soft-boiled eggs in half and place them on top of the asparagus.
8. Garnish with fresh parsley and serve with lemon wedges if desired.

Low-Phosphorus Bran Muffins with Apple Compote

2 servings | **40 minutes**

Cal 180
Fat 7 g
Carb 30 g
Protein 4 g
Sodium 160 mg
Potassium 180 mg
Phosphorus 70 mg

INGREDIENTS

For Bran Muffins:
- 1 cup oat bran
- 1/2 cup whole wheat flour
- 1/4 cup ground flaxseed
- 1 teaspoon baking powder
- 1/2 teaspoon baking soda
- 1/4 teaspoon salt
- 1/2 cup unsweetened applesauce
- 1/4 cup honey or maple syrup
- 1/4 cup vegetable oil
- 2/3 cup low-fat buttermilk
- 1 large egg
- 1 teaspoon vanilla extract

For Apple Compote:
- 2 medium apples, peeled, cored, and diced
- 2 tablespoons water
- 1 tablespoon honey or maple syrup
- 1/2 teaspoon cinnamon

DIRECTIONS

For Bran Muffins:
1. Preheat the oven to 375°F (190°C). Line a muffin tin with paper liners or grease each cup.
2. In a large bowl, combine oat bran, whole wheat flour, ground flaxseed, baking powder, baking soda, and salt.
3. In a separate bowl, whisk together applesauce, honey or maple syrup, vegetable oil, buttermilk, egg, and vanilla extract.
4. Add the wet ingredients to the dry ingredients, stirring until just combined. Do not overmix.
5. Divide the batter evenly among the muffin cups.
6. Bake for 15-18 minutes or until a toothpick inserted into the center comes out clean.
7. Allow the muffins to cool in the tin for 5 minutes, then transfer them to a wire rack to cool completely.

For Apple Compote:
8. In a saucepan, combine diced apples, water, honey or maple syrup, and cinnamon.
9. Bring the mixture to a simmer over medium heat.
10. Reduce heat to low and let it simmer for about 10 minutes or until the apples are soft and the liquid has thickened slightly.
11. Remove from heat and let the compote cool.

Assembly:
12. Once the muffins are cooled, top each with a spoonful of apple compote.
13. Serve and enjoy these delicious low-phosphorus bran muffins with apple compote.

Tomato and Cucumber Breakfast Salad with Feta Cheese

2 servings | 15 minutes

Cal 120
Fat 8 g
Carb 10 g
Protein 3 g
Sodium 160 mg
Potassium 300 mg
Phosphorus 80 mg

INGREDIENTS

- 1 cup cherry tomatoes, halved
- 1 cucumber, diced
- 1/4 cup red onion, finely chopped
- 2 tablespoons fresh parsley, chopped
- 2 tablespoons feta cheese, crumbled
- 1 tablespoon olive oil
- 1 tablespoon balsamic vinegar
- Salt and pepper to taste
- 2 poached eggs (optional, for added protein)

DIRECTIONS

1. In a large bowl, combine cherry tomatoes, diced cucumber, chopped red onion, and fresh parsley.
2. In a small bowl, whisk together olive oil and balsamic vinegar. Pour the dressing over the vegetables and toss gently to coat.
3. Sprinkle crumbled feta cheese over the salad.
4. Season with salt and pepper to taste. Toss again to combine.
5. If desired, top the salad with poached eggs for added protein.

Brown Rice Porridge with Cinnamon and Raisins

2 servings | 60 minutes

Cal 250
Fat 3 g
Carb 50 g
Protein 5 g

Sodium 60 mg
Potassium 200 mg
Phosphorus 140 mg

INGREDIENTS

- 1/2 cup brown rice, rinsed
- 2 cups water
- 1 cup low-fat milk or a dairy-free alternative
- 1 tablespoon honey or maple syrup
- 1/2 teaspoon ground cinnamon
- 1/4 cup raisins
- Chopped nuts (e.g., almonds or walnuts) for topping (optional)

DIRECTIONS

1. In a saucepan, combine brown rice and water. Bring to a boil, then reduce the heat to low, cover, and simmer for 45-50 minutes or until the rice is tender and most of the liquid is absorbed.
2. Stir in low-fat milk (or dairy-free alternative), honey (or maple syrup), ground cinnamon, and raisins.
3. Continue to simmer the mixture over low heat for an additional 10-15 minutes, stirring occasionally, until the porridge reaches a creamy consistency.
4. Adjust sweetness and cinnamon to taste.
5. Remove the brown rice porridge from heat and let it stand for a few minutes to thicken.
6. Serve the porridge hot, topped with chopped nuts if desired.

Egg and Vegetable Breakfast Burrito with Whole Wheat Tortilla

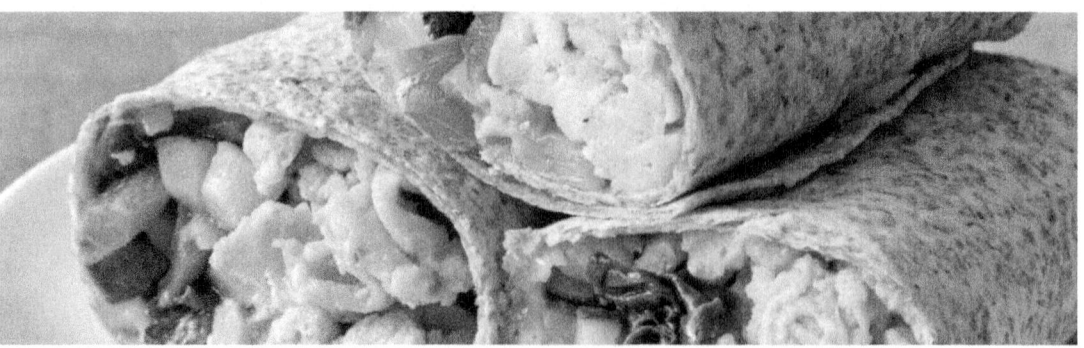

2 servings | 15 minutes

Cal 350
Fat 15 g
Carb 40 g
Protein 15 g
Sodium 400 mg
Potassium 450 mg
Phosphorus 250 mg

INGREDIENTS

- 2 large eggs, beaten
- 1/2 cup bell peppers, diced (assorted colors)
- 1/4 cup red onion, finely chopped
- 1/4 cup cherry tomatoes, diced
- 1/4 cup spinach, chopped
- 2 whole wheat tortillas (8-inch)
- 1/4 cup shredded low-fat cheese (optional)
- 1 tablespoon olive oil
- Salt and pepper to taste
- Salsa or hot sauce for serving (optional)

DIRECTIONS

1. In a skillet, heat olive oil over medium heat.
2. Add diced bell peppers and red onion to the skillet. Sauté until vegetables are softened.
3. Add cherry tomatoes and chopped spinach to the skillet. Cook for an additional 2-3 minutes until the spinach wilts.
4. Push the vegetables to the side of the skillet, creating a space for the eggs.
5. Pour beaten eggs into the empty side of the skillet. Season with salt and pepper.
6. Scramble the eggs and mix them with the sautéed vegetables until the eggs are fully cooked.
7. If using, sprinkle shredded low-fat cheese over the egg and vegetable mixture. Allow it to melt.
8. Warm the whole wheat tortillas in a dry skillet or microwave.
9. Divide the egg and vegetable mixture evenly between the tortillas.
10. Roll up the tortillas, folding the sides in to create a burrito.
11. Serve the Egg and Vegetable Breakfast Burritos with salsa or hot sauce if desired.

Low-Sodium Turkey Sausage with Sweet Potato Hash

2 servings | 35 minutes

Cal 300
Fat 15 g
Carb 25 g
Protein 20 g

Sodium 150 mg
Potassium 480 mg
Phosphorus 220 mg

INGREDIENTS

For Turkey Sausage:
- 1/2 lb lean ground turkey
- 1 teaspoon fennel seeds
- 1/2 teaspoon dried sage
- 1/2 teaspoon dried thyme
- 1/2 teaspoon garlic powder
- 1/4 teaspoon black pepper
- 1 tablespoon olive oil for cooking

For Sweet Potato Hash:
- 2 medium sweet potatoes, peeled and diced
- 1/2 onion, finely chopped
- 1 bell pepper (any color), diced
- 1 tablespoon olive oil
- Salt and pepper to taste
- Fresh parsley for garnish (optional)

DIRECTIONS

For Turkey Sausage:
1. In a bowl, combine ground turkey with fennel seeds, dried sage, dried thyme, garlic powder, and black pepper. Mix well.
2. Form the turkey mixture into small patties.
3. Heat olive oil in a skillet over medium heat.
4. Cook the turkey sausage patties for 4-5 minutes on each side or until fully cooked.

For Sweet Potato Hash:
5. In a large skillet, heat olive oil over medium heat.
6. Add chopped onion and diced bell pepper to the skillet. Sauté until vegetables are softened.
7. Add diced sweet potatoes to the skillet. Cook for 10-12 minutes or until the sweet potatoes are tender, stirring occasionally.
8. Season the sweet potato hash with salt and pepper to taste.
9. Once the sweet potatoes are cooked through, transfer the hash to serving plates.
10. Top the sweet potato hash with the cooked turkey sausage patties.
11. Garnish with fresh parsley if desired.

Cherry Almond Breakfast Quinoa

2 servings | 35 minutes

Cal 320
Fat 8 g
Carb 50 g
Protein 12 g

Sodium 90 mg
Potassium 380 mg
Phosphorus 280 mg

INGREDIENTS

- 1 cup quinoa, rinsed
- 2 cups water
- 1 cup low-fat milk or a dairy-free alternative
- 1/4 cup dried cherries, chopped
- 2 tablespoons almonds, sliced
- 1 tablespoon honey or maple syrup
- 1/2 teaspoon almond extract
- Fresh cherries for garnish (optional)

DIRECTIONS

1. In a medium saucepan, combine quinoa and water. Bring to a boil, then reduce the heat to low, cover, and simmer for 15-20 minutes or until the quinoa is cooked and the water is absorbed.
2. Stir in low-fat milk (or dairy-free alternative), dried cherries, sliced almonds, honey (or maple syrup), and almond extract.
3. Continue to simmer the mixture over low heat for an additional 5-7 minutes, stirring occasionally, until it reaches a creamy consistency.
4. Adjust sweetness and almond flavor to taste.
5. Remove the Cherry Almond Breakfast Quinoa from heat.
6. Serve the quinoa hot, garnished with fresh cherries if desired.

Spinach and Mushroom Breakfast Quesadilla

2 servings | 15 minutes

Cal 350
Fat 18 g
Carb 30 g
Protein 18 g

Sodium 350 mg
Potassium 400 mg
Phosphorus 240 mg

INGREDIENTS

- 2 whole wheat tortillas (8-inch)
- 1 cup fresh spinach, chopped
- 1/2 cup mushrooms, sliced
- 2 eggs, beaten
- 1/4 cup low-fat shredded cheese (e.g., mozzarella or cheddar)
- 1 tablespoon olive oil
- Salt and pepper to taste
- Salsa or Greek yogurt for serving (optional)

DIRECTIONS

1. In a skillet, heat olive oil over medium heat.
2. Add sliced mushrooms to the skillet and sauté until they release their moisture and become golden brown.
3. Add chopped spinach to the skillet and cook until wilted. Season with salt and pepper.
4. Push the vegetables to one side of the skillet and pour beaten eggs into the empty side. Scramble the eggs until fully cooked.
5. Combine the cooked vegetables with the scrambled eggs in the skillet. Mix well.
6. Place one whole wheat tortilla in the skillet.
7. Spread half of the egg and vegetable mixture evenly over one half of the tortilla.
8. Sprinkle half of the shredded cheese over the egg and vegetable mixture.
9. Fold the other half of the tortilla over the filling, creating a semi-circle.
10. Press down gently with a spatula and cook for 2-3 minutes on each side, or until the tortilla is golden brown and the cheese is melted.
11. Repeat the process for the second quesadilla.
12. Serve the Spinach and Mushroom Breakfast Quesadillas with salsa or Greek yogurt if desired.

Homemade Low-Phosphorus Scones with Berries

2 servings | 35 minutes

Cal 180
Fat 10 g
Carb 20 g
Protein 3 g
Sodium 130 mg
Potassium 60 mg
Phosphorus 60 mg

INGREDIENTS

- 1 1/2 cups all-purpose flour
- 1/2 cup almond flour
- 1/4 cup granulated sugar (or a sugar substitute)
- 2 teaspoons baking powder
- 1/2 teaspoon baking soda
- 1/4 teaspoon salt
- 1/2 cup unsalted butter, cold and cubed
- 1/2 cup buttermilk
- 1 teaspoon vanilla extract
- 1/2 cup mixed berries (e.g., blueberries, raspberries)
- 1 tablespoon lemon zest (optional)
- 1 tablespoon powdered sugar for dusting (optional)

DIRECTIONS

1. Preheat the oven to 400°F (200°C). Line a baking sheet with parchment paper.
2. In a large mixing bowl, combine all-purpose flour, almond flour, sugar, baking powder, baking soda, and salt.
3. Add the cold, cubed butter to the dry ingredients. Use a pastry cutter or your fingers to cut the butter into the flour until the mixture resembles coarse crumbs.
4. In a separate bowl, mix buttermilk and vanilla extract.
5. Pour the buttermilk mixture into the flour-butter mixture. Stir until just combined.
6. Gently fold in the mixed berries and lemon zest, being careful not to overmix.
7. Turn the dough out onto a floured surface and pat it into a circle about 1 inch thick.
8. Use a round cutter to cut out scones from the dough. Place them on the prepared baking sheet.
9. Bake for 12-15 minutes or until the scones are golden brown.
10. Allow the scones to cool on a wire rack.
11. If desired, dust the cooled scones with powdered sugar before serving.

Cauliflower Hash Browns with Poached Eggs

2 servings | 30 minutes

Cal 180
Fat 10 g
Carb 20 g
Protein 3 g

Sodium 130 mg
Potassium 60 mg
Phosphorus 60 mg

INGREDIENTS

For Cauliflower Hash Browns:
- 2 cups cauliflower florets, grated or finely chopped
- 1/4 cup onion, finely chopped
- 1/4 cup bell pepper, finely chopped
- 1/4 cup Parmesan cheese, grated
- 2 tablespoons almond flour
- 1 large egg
- 1/2 teaspoon garlic powder
- 1/2 teaspoon onion powder
- Salt and pepper to taste
- 2 tablespoons olive oil for cooking

For Poached Eggs:
- 4 large eggs
- Water for poaching
- 1 tablespoon white vinegar (optional, for poaching)

DIRECTIONS

For Cauliflower Hash Browns:
1. In a large bowl, combine grated cauliflower, chopped onion, chopped bell pepper, Parmesan cheese, almond flour, egg, garlic powder, onion powder, salt, and pepper.
2. Mix the ingredients until well combined.
3. Heat olive oil in a skillet over medium heat.
4. Scoop portions of the cauliflower mixture and form them into patties. Place the patties in the hot skillet.
5. Cook the cauliflower hash browns for 4-5 minutes on each side or until they are golden brown and cooked through.
6. Remove from the skillet and set aside.

For Poached Eggs:
7. Fill a wide saucepan with water, about 2-3 inches deep. Add white vinegar if using.
8. Bring the water to a gentle simmer over medium heat.
9. Crack each egg into a small bowl.
10. Create a gentle whirlpool in the simmering water by stirring with a spoon. Carefully slide the eggs, one at a time, into the center of the whirlpool.
11. Poach the eggs for about 3-4 minutes for a runny yolk or longer if desired.
12. Use a slotted spoon to remove the poached eggs from the water.

Assembly:
13. Place cauliflower hash browns on a plate.
14. Top each hash brown with a poached egg.
15. Season with salt and pepper to taste.
16. Serve the Cauliflower Hash Browns with Poached Eggs hot.
17. Enjoy this wholesome and flavorful breakfast.

Papaya Boat with Cottage Cheese and Lime

2 servings | 5 minutes

Cal 250
Fat 2 g
Carb 40 g
Protein 20 g

Sodium 300 mg
Potassium 900 mg
Phosphorus 300 mg

INGREDIENTS

- 1 medium-sized ripe papaya, halved and seeds removed
- 1 cup low-fat cottage cheese
- Zest and juice of 1 lime
- 1 tablespoon honey or maple syrup (optional)
- Fresh mint leaves for garnish

DIRECTIONS

1. Scoop out a portion of the papaya flesh to create a well in each papaya half.
2. In a bowl, mix together low-fat cottage cheese, lime zest, and lime juice. Add honey or maple syrup if desired, adjusting sweetness to taste.
3. Spoon the cottage cheese mixture into the well of each papaya half.
4. Garnish with fresh mint leaves.
5. Serve the Papaya Boat with Cottage Cheese and Lime immediately.
6. Enjoy this refreshing and nutrient-packed snack or light dessert.

Low-Phosphorus Bran Flakes with Low-Potassium Berries

2 servings | 5 minutes

Cal 250
Fat 8 g
Carb 40 g
Protein 10 g

Sodium 100 mg
Potassium 250 mg
Phosphorus 180 mg

INGREDIENTS
- 1 cup low-phosphorus bran flakes cereal
- 1/2 cup low-fat milk or a dairy-free alternative
- 1/2 cup mixed berries (e.g., strawberries, blueberries, raspberries)
- 1 tablespoon chia seeds (optional)
- 1 tablespoon chopped nuts (e.g., almonds or walnuts)
- 1 teaspoon honey or maple syrup (optional)

DIRECTIONS
1. In a bowl, combine low-phosphorus bran flakes cereal and low-fat milk (or dairy-free alternative).
2. Allow the cereal to soak for a few minutes until it reaches your desired consistency.
3. Add mixed berries, chia seeds (if using), and chopped nuts to the cereal.
4. Drizzle with honey or maple syrup if additional sweetness is desired.
5. Gently mix the ingredients together.
6. Serve the Low-Phosphorus Bran Flakes with Low-Potassium Berries immediately.

Smoked Salmon Wrap with Cream Cheese and Cucumber

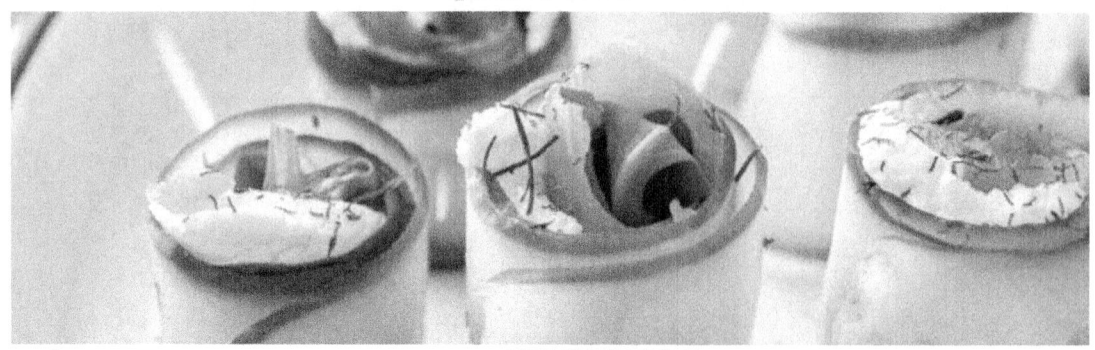

2 servings | 15 minutes

Cal 300
Fat 15 g
Carb 20 g
Protein 20 g

Sodium 550 mg
Potassium 200 mg
Phosphorus 250 mg

INGREDIENTS

- 2 whole wheat or low-phosphorus wraps
- 4 ounces smoked salmon
- 1/2 cup low-fat cream cheese
- 1/2 cucumber, thinly sliced
- 1 tablespoon capers, drained
- Fresh dill for garnish
- Lemon wedges for serving

DIRECTIONS

1. Lay out the wraps on a clean surface or plate.
2. Spread a generous layer of low-fat cream cheese evenly over each wrap.
3. Place slices of smoked salmon on top of the cream cheese, covering the entire surface of the wrap.
4. Arrange thinly sliced cucumber over the smoked salmon.
5. Sprinkle capers evenly over the cucumber.
6. Garnish with fresh dill.
7. Carefully fold the sides of the wraps and then roll them up tightly, creating a wrap.
8. If desired, slice the wraps in half diagonally for easier handling.
9. Serve the Smoked Salmon Wrap with Cream Cheese and Cucumber with lemon wedges on the side.

Lunch

Grilled Chicken Salad with Mixed Greens

2 servings | 20 minutes

Cal 400
Fat 20 g
Carb 25 g
Protein 30 g

Sodium 350 mg
Potassium 500 mg
Phosphorus 250 mg

INGREDIENTS

- 2 boneless, skinless chicken breasts
- 6 cups mixed salad greens (spinach, arugula, romaine)
- 1 cup cherry tomatoes, halved
- 1 cucumber, sliced
- 1/2 red onion, thinly sliced
- 1/4 cup crumbled feta cheese (optional)
- 2 tablespoons extra-virgin olive oil
- 2 tablespoons balsamic vinegar
- 1 teaspoon Dijon mustard
- Salt and pepper to taste

DIRECTIONS

1. Preheat the grill to medium-high heat.
2. Season chicken breasts with a pinch of salt and pepper.
3. Grill chicken for 6-8 minutes per side until fully cooked (internal temperature reaches 165°F or 74°C).
4. Allow chicken to rest for a few minutes before slicing into thin strips.
5. In a large bowl, combine mixed salad greens, cherry tomatoes, cucumber, and red onion.
6. In a small bowl, whisk together olive oil, balsamic vinegar, Dijon mustard, and a dash of salt and pepper.
7. Divide the salad mixture between two plates.
8. Top each salad with sliced grilled chicken and crumbled feta cheese (if using).
9. Drizzle the balsamic vinaigrette over each salad just before serving.

Lemon Herb Baked Cod with Quinoa and Steamed Broccoli

2 servings | 40 minutes

Cal 350
Fat 10 g
Carb 35 g
Protein 30 g

Sodium 200 mg
Potassium 400 mg
Phosphorus 250 mg

INGREDIENTS

- 4 cod fillets (about 6 ounces each)
- 1 cup quinoa, rinsed
- 2 cups broccoli florets
- 2 tablespoons olive oil
- 2 tablespoons fresh lemon juice
- 1 teaspoon lemon zest
- 2 cloves garlic, minced
- 1 tablespoon fresh parsley, chopped
- 1 teaspoon dried oregano
- Salt and pepper to taste

DIRECTIONS

1. Preheat the oven to 375°F (190°C).
2. Pat dry 4 cod fillets (about 6 ounces each) and place them in a baking dish lined with parchment paper. Drizzle with 1 tablespoon of olive oil and lemon juice. Season with minced garlic, dried oregano, salt, and pepper. Sprinkle lemon zest over the fillets.
3. Bake the cod in the preheated oven for 15-20 minutes or until the fish flakes easily with a fork.
4. While the cod is baking, rinse 1 cup of quinoa under cold water. In a medium saucepan, combine quinoa with 2 cups of water. Bring to a boil, then reduce heat to low, cover, and simmer for 15 minutes or until the quinoa is cooked and water is absorbed.
5. In a steamer basket over boiling water, steam 2 cups of broccoli florets for about 5-7 minutes or until tender-crisp.
6. Fluff the cooked quinoa with a fork and divide it among four plates. Place a baked cod fillet on top of each quinoa bed. Arrange steamed broccoli around the cod.
7. In a small bowl, mix the remaining 1 tablespoon of olive oil with chopped parsley. Drizzle the herb sauce over the cod and quinoa.

Vegetarian Chickpea and Spinach Curry with Brown Rice

2 servings   **40 minutes**

Cal 400
Fat 10 g
Carb 65 g
Protein 15 g

Sodium 300 mg
Potassium 500 mg
Phosphorus 200 mg

INGREDIENTS

- 2 cups cooked chickpeas (canned or pre-cooked)
- 1 onion, finely chopped
- 2 cloves garlic, minced
- 1 tablespoon ginger, grated
- 1 can (14 ounces) diced tomatoes
- 1 can (14 ounces) coconut milk
- 4 cups fresh spinach, washed and chopped
- 2 tablespoons curry powder
- 1 teaspoon ground cumin
- 1 teaspoon ground coriander
- 1 tablespoon olive oil
- Salt and pepper to taste
- 2 cups cooked brown rice

DIRECTIONS

1. In a large pan, heat olive oil over medium heat. Add chopped onion, minced garlic, and grated ginger. Sauté until the onion is translucent.
2. Stir in curry powder, ground cumin, and ground coriander. Cook for an additional 2 minutes, allowing the spices to release their flavors.
3. Add diced tomatoes (with juice) and cooked chickpeas to the pan. Simmer for 10 minutes, allowing the flavors to meld.
4. Pour in the coconut milk and add chopped spinach. Stir well and let it simmer for an additional 5-7 minutes until the spinach wilts.
5. Season the curry with salt and pepper to taste. Adjust the seasoning as needed.
6. Serve the Vegetarian Chickpea and Spinach Curry over cooked brown rice.
7. Garnish with fresh cilantro or a squeeze of lime juice before serving.

Tuna Salad Lettuce Wraps with Cherry Tomatoes

2 servings | 15 minutes

Cal 250
Fat 10 g
Carb 10 g
Protein 25 g

Sodium 350 mg
Potassium 300 mg
Phosphorus 150 mg

INGREDIENTS

- 2 cans (5 ounces each) tuna in water, drained
- 1/2 cup celery, finely chopped
- 1/4 cup red onion, finely chopped
- 1/4 cup mayonnaise (low-fat or light)
- 1 tablespoon Dijon mustard
- 1 tablespoon lemon juice
- Salt and pepper to taste
- 8 large lettuce leaves (such as iceberg or butterhead)
- 1 cup cherry tomatoes, halved

DIRECTIONS

1. In a bowl, combine drained tuna, chopped celery, finely chopped red onion, mayonnaise, Dijon mustard, and lemon juice. Mix well.
2. Season the tuna salad with salt and pepper to taste. Adjust the seasoning as needed.
3. Spoon the tuna salad onto each lettuce leaf, distributing it evenly.
4. Top each tuna-filled lettuce leaf with halved cherry tomatoes for a burst of freshness.
5. Gently fold the lettuce leaves around the tuna salad and cherry tomatoes to create wraps.
6. Serve the Tuna Salad Lettuce Wraps with Cherry Tomatoes immediately for a light and refreshing meal.

Eggplant and Zucchini Lasagna with Ground Turkey

2 servings | 35 minutes

Cal 400
Fat 15 g
Carb 35 g
Protein 25 g
Sodium 400 mg
Potassium 450 mg
Phosphorus 300 mg

INGREDIENTS

- 1 pound ground turkey
- 1 large eggplant, sliced
- 2 medium zucchinis, sliced
- 1 onion, finely chopped
- 2 cloves garlic, minced
- 1 can (14 ounces) crushed tomatoes
- 1 can (14 ounces) tomato sauce
- 1 teaspoon dried oregano
- 1 teaspoon dried basil
- Salt and pepper to taste
- 2 cups ricotta cheese
- 1 cup shredded mozzarella cheese
- 1/2 cup grated Parmesan cheese
- Fresh basil for garnish (optional)

DIRECTIONS

1. In a large skillet, brown the ground turkey over medium heat. Drain any excess fat.
2. Add chopped onion and minced garlic to the skillet. Cook until the onion is translucent.
3. Stir in crushed tomatoes, tomato sauce, dried oregano, dried basil, salt, and pepper. Simmer for 10-15 minutes.
4. Preheat the oven to 375°F (190°C).
5. In a separate pan, grill the eggplant and zucchini slices until they are slightly softened.
6. In a greased baking dish, layer the eggplant and zucchini slices, followed by a layer of the turkey-tomato sauce mixture.
7. Spread a layer of ricotta cheese over the turkey-tomato sauce mixture, and then sprinkle with mozzarella and Parmesan cheese.
8. Repeat the layers until the baking dish is filled, finishing with a layer of cheese on top.
9. Bake in the preheated oven for 30-35 minutes, or until the cheese is golden and bubbly.
10. Allow the lasagna to rest for 10 minutes before serving.
11. Garnish with fresh basil if desired.

Salmon and Asparagus Foil Packets with Lemon

2 servings | 20 minutes

Cal 300
Fat 15 g
Carb 10 g
Protein 30 g
Sodium 200 mg
Potassium 500 mg
Phosphorus 300 mg

INGREDIENTS
- 4 salmon fillets (about 6 ounces each)
- 1 bunch asparagus, trimmed
- 2 tablespoons olive oil
- 2 tablespoons fresh lemon juice
- 2 cloves garlic, minced
- 1 teaspoon dried dill
- Salt and pepper to taste
- Lemon slices for garnish

DIRECTIONS
1. Preheat the oven to 400°F (200°C).
2. Cut four large pieces of aluminum foil.
3. Place a salmon fillet in the center of each piece of foil.
4. Arrange asparagus around each salmon fillet.
5. In a small bowl, whisk together olive oil, lemon juice, minced garlic, dried dill, salt, and pepper.
6. Drizzle the olive oil mixture evenly over the salmon and asparagus.
7. Fold the sides of the foil over the salmon and asparagus, creating sealed packets.
8. Place the foil packets on a baking sheet and bake in the preheated oven for 15-20 minutes, or until the salmon is cooked through and flakes easily with a fork.
9. Carefully open the foil packets, being cautious of the steam.
10. Garnish with lemon slices and serve immediately.

Mediterranean Chickpea and Vegetable Bowl

2 servings — **35 minutes**

Cal 350
Fat 10 g
Carb 55 g
Protein 15 g

Sodium 300 mg
Potassium 450 mg
Phosphorus 200 mg

INGREDIENTS

- 1 can (15 ounces) chickpeas, drained and rinsed
- 1 cup cherry tomatoes, halved
- 1 cucumber, diced
- 1 red bell pepper, diced
- 1/2 red onion, finely chopped
- 1/4 cup Kalamata olives, sliced
- 1/4 cup feta cheese, crumbled
- 2 tablespoons extra-virgin olive oil
- 1 tablespoon red wine vinegar
- 1 teaspoon dried oregano
- Salt and pepper to taste
- Fresh parsley for garnish (optional)

DIRECTIONS

1. In a large mixing bowl, combine chickpeas, cherry tomatoes, cucumber, red bell pepper, red onion, Kalamata olives, and feta cheese.
2. In a small bowl, whisk together extra-virgin olive oil, red wine vinegar, dried oregano, salt, and pepper to create the dressing.
3. Pour the dressing over the chickpea and vegetable mixture. Toss until well combined.
4. Allow the bowl to marinate in the refrigerator for at least 30 minutes to let the flavors meld.
5. Before serving, garnish with fresh parsley if desired.

Turkey and Vegetable Stir-Fry with Quinoa

2 servings | 25 minutes

Cal 400
Fat 15 g
Carb 40 g
Protein 30 g

Sodium 350 mg
Potassium 500 mg
Phosphorus 250 mg

INGREDIENTS
- 1 pound ground turkey
- 1 cup quinoa, rinsed
- 2 cups broccoli florets
- 1 bell pepper (any color), thinly sliced
- 1 carrot, julienned
- 1 zucchini, sliced
- 2 tablespoons soy sauce (low-sodium)
- 1 tablespoon hoisin sauce
- 1 tablespoon sesame oil
- 2 cloves garlic, minced
- 1 tablespoon ginger, grated
- 2 green onions, sliced
- Sesame seeds for garnish (optional)

DIRECTIONS
1. In a medium saucepan, combine quinoa with 2 cups of water. Bring to a boil, then reduce heat to low, cover, and simmer for 15 minutes or until the quinoa is cooked and water is absorbed.
2. In a wok or large skillet, brown the ground turkey over medium-high heat. Break it into crumbles as it cooks.
3. Add minced garlic and grated ginger to the turkey, and cook for an additional 2 minutes until fragrant.
4. Add broccoli, bell pepper, carrot, and zucchini to the wok. Stir-fry for 5-7 minutes until the vegetables are tender-crisp.
5. In a small bowl, mix soy sauce, hoisin sauce, and sesame oil. Pour the sauce over the turkey and vegetables. Toss to coat evenly.
6. Add cooked quinoa to the stir-fry mixture and stir until everything is well combined.
7. Cook for an additional 2-3 minutes to heat through.
8. Garnish with sliced green onions and sesame seeds if desired.

Shrimp and Avocado Salad with Lime Dressing

2 servings | 20 minutes

Cal 300
Fat 20 g
Carb 15 g
Protein 20 g
Sodium 300 mg
Potassium 400 mg
Phosphorus 200 mg

INGREDIENTS

- 1 pound large shrimp, peeled and deveined
- 2 avocados, diced
- 1 cup cherry tomatoes, halved
- 1 cucumber, diced
- 1/4 cup red onion, finely chopped
- 1/4 cup fresh cilantro, chopped
- 2 tablespoons extra-virgin olive oil
- Juice of 2 limes
- 1 teaspoon honey
- 1 clove garlic, minced
- Salt and pepper to taste
- Mixed salad greens for serving

DIRECTIONS

1. In a large skillet, cook the shrimp over medium-high heat for 2-3 minutes per side or until they turn pink and opaque. Set aside to cool.
2. In a large salad bowl, combine diced avocados, cherry tomatoes, diced cucumber, chopped red onion, and fresh cilantro.
3. In a small bowl, whisk together extra-virgin olive oil, lime juice, honey, minced garlic, salt, and pepper to create the dressing.
4. Add the cooked shrimp to the salad bowl.
5. Pour the lime dressing over the salad and shrimp. Toss gently to coat everything evenly.
6. Serve the shrimp and avocado salad over a bed of mixed salad greens.
7. Garnish with additional cilantro if desired.

Roasted Vegetable and Lentil Soup

2 servings | 30 minutes

Cal 300
Fat 5 g
Carb 50 g
Protein 15 g

Sodium 400 mg
Potassium 600 mg
Phosphorus 200 mg

INGREDIENTS

- 1 cup dry green or brown lentils, rinsed and drained
- 1 large sweet potato, peeled and diced
- 2 carrots, peeled and sliced
- 1 zucchini, diced
- 1 red bell pepper, diced
- 1 onion, chopped
- 3 cloves garlic, minced
- 2 tablespoons olive oil
- 1 teaspoon ground cumin
- 1 teaspoon paprika
- 1/2 teaspoon ground coriander
- Salt and pepper to taste
- 6 cups vegetable broth
- 1 can (14 ounces) diced tomatoes, undrained
- 2 cups kale or spinach, chopped
- Juice of 1 lemon
- Fresh parsley for garnish (optional)

DIRECTIONS

1. Preheat the oven to 400°F (200°C).
2. In a large mixing bowl, combine diced sweet potato, sliced carrots, diced zucchini, diced red bell pepper, chopped onion, and minced garlic.
3. Drizzle olive oil over the vegetables and toss to coat. Sprinkle ground cumin, paprika, ground coriander, salt, and pepper over the vegetables. Toss again to evenly distribute the spices.
4. Spread the seasoned vegetables on a baking sheet in a single layer. Roast in the preheated oven for 25-30 minutes or until the vegetables are tender and lightly browned, stirring halfway through.
5. In a large pot, combine rinsed lentils, vegetable broth, and diced tomatoes (undrained). Bring to a boil, then reduce heat to low and simmer for 20-25 minutes or until the lentils are tender.
6. Add the roasted vegetables and chopped kale or spinach to the pot. Simmer for an additional 5-7 minutes.
7. Stir in the lemon juice and season with additional salt and pepper if needed.
8. Serve the Roasted Vegetable and Lentil Soup hot, garnished with fresh parsley if desired.

Caprese Chicken Skewers with Basil Pesto

2 servings | 25 minutes

Cal 350
Fat 20 g
Carb 5 g
Protein 30 g
Sodium 350 mg
Potassium 300 mg
Phosphorus 200 mg

INGREDIENTS

- 1 pound boneless, skinless chicken breasts, cut into bite-sized cubes
- 1 pint cherry tomatoes
- 8 ounces fresh mozzarella balls
- Fresh basil leaves
- 2 tablespoons olive oil
- Salt and pepper to taste
- Wooden skewers, soaked in water for 30 minutes
- Basil pesto for drizzling

DIRECTIONS

1. Preheat the grill or grill pan over medium-high heat.
2. In a bowl, toss the chicken cubes with olive oil, salt, and pepper.
3. Thread the marinated chicken, cherry tomatoes, fresh mozzarella balls, and basil leaves onto the soaked wooden skewers, alternating the ingredients.
4. Grill the skewers for 10-12 minutes, turning occasionally, until the chicken is cooked through and has a nice char.
5. Once the skewers are cooked, arrange them on a serving platter.
6. Drizzle basil pesto over the skewers just before serving.
7. Serve the Caprese Chicken Skewers with Basil Pesto immediately, either as an appetizer or a main dish.

Cauliflower Rice and Black Bean Bowl with Salsa

2 servings | 25 minutes

Cal 300
Fat 10 g
Carb 45 g
Protein 15 g

Sodium 350 mg
Potassium 400 mg
Phosphorus 250 mg

INGREDIENTS

- 1 medium-sized cauliflower, grated (or store-bought cauliflower rice)
- 1 can (15 ounces) black beans, drained and rinsed
- 1 cup corn kernels (fresh or frozen)
- 1 red bell pepper, diced
- 1 avocado, sliced
- 1/2 red onion, finely chopped
- Fresh cilantro leaves for garnish
- Lime wedges for serving

For Salsa:
- 2 tomatoes, diced
- 1/4 cup red onion, finely chopped
- 1 jalapeño, seeds removed and finely chopped
- 1/4 cup fresh cilantro, chopped
- Juice of 1 lime
- Salt and pepper to taste

DIRECTIONS

1. In a large skillet, sauté the grated cauliflower over medium heat for 5-7 minutes, or until it reaches a rice-like consistency. Set aside.
2. In the same skillet, warm the black beans, corn kernels, and diced red bell pepper over medium heat for 5 minutes.
3. In a medium bowl, combine diced tomatoes, chopped red onion, chopped jalapeño, fresh cilantro, lime juice, salt, and pepper to make the salsa. Set aside.
4. Assemble the bowls by dividing the cauliflower rice among serving dishes.
5. Top the cauliflower rice with the warm black bean and vegetable mixture.
6. Garnish with sliced avocado, finely chopped red onion, and fresh cilantro leaves.
7. Drizzle salsa generously over each bowl.
8. Serve the Cauliflower Rice and Black Bean Bowl with Salsa with lime wedges on the side.

Spinach and Feta Stuffed Chicken Breast with Roasted Brussels Sprouts

2 servings | 35 minutes

Cal 400
Fat 20 g
Carb 15 g
Protein 35 g
Sodium 350 mg
Potassium 500 mg
Phosphorus 300 mg

INGREDIENTS

For Stuffed Chicken Breast:
- 4 boneless, skinless chicken breasts
- 2 cups fresh spinach, chopped
- 1/2 cup feta cheese, crumbled
- 1 clove garlic, minced
- 1 tablespoon olive oil
- Salt and pepper to taste
- Toothpicks or kitchen twine

For Roasted Brussels Sprouts:
- 1 pound Brussels sprouts, trimmed and halved
- 2 tablespoons olive oil
- 1 teaspoon garlic powder
- Salt and pepper to taste

DIRECTIONS

For Stuffed Chicken Breast:
1. Preheat the oven to 375°F (190°C).
2. In a skillet, sauté chopped spinach and minced garlic in olive oil over medium heat until the spinach is wilted. Remove from heat and let it cool.
3. Butterfly each chicken breast by slicing horizontally, leaving the edges intact.
4. Season the inside of each chicken breast with salt and pepper.
5. Stuff each chicken breast with the sautéed spinach and garlic mixture, and then add crumbled feta.
6. Secure the stuffed chicken breasts with toothpicks or tie them with kitchen twine.
7. Season the outside of each chicken breast with salt and pepper.
8. In an oven-safe skillet, heat olive oil over medium-high heat. Sear the stuffed chicken breasts on both sides until browned.
9. Transfer the skillet to the preheated oven and bake for 20-25 minutes or until the chicken is cooked through.

For Roasted Brussels Sprouts:
10. While the chicken is baking, preheat the oven to 400°F (200°C).
11. In a bowl, toss halved Brussels sprouts with olive oil, garlic powder, salt, and pepper.
12. Spread the Brussels sprouts on a baking sheet in a single layer.
13. Roast in the preheated oven for 20-25 minutes, or until the Brussels sprouts are golden and crispy on the edges.

Quinoa and Black-Eyed Pea Salad with Herbs

2 servings | 35 minutes

Cal 350
Fat 10 g
Carb 50 g
Protein 15 g
Sodium 300 mg
Potassium 400 mg
Phosphorus 250 mg

INGREDIENTS

- 1 cup quinoa, rinsed
- 2 cups cooked black-eyed peas (canned or pre-cooked)
- 1 cucumber, diced
- 1 red bell pepper, diced
- 1/2 red onion, finely chopped
- 1/4 cup fresh parsley, chopped
- 1/4 cup fresh mint, chopped
- 1/4 cup olive oil
- 2 tablespoons red wine vinegar
- Juice of 1 lemon
- 1 teaspoon Dijon mustard
- Salt and pepper to taste

DIRECTIONS

1. In a medium saucepan, combine quinoa with 2 cups of water. Bring to a boil, then reduce heat to low, cover, and simmer for 15 minutes or until the quinoa is cooked and water is absorbed.
2. In a large mixing bowl, combine cooked quinoa, black-eyed peas, diced cucumber, diced red bell pepper, finely chopped red onion, fresh parsley, and fresh mint.
3. In a small bowl, whisk together olive oil, red wine vinegar, lemon juice, Dijon mustard, salt, and pepper to create the dressing.
4. Pour the dressing over the quinoa and black-eyed pea mixture. Toss until everything is well coated.
5. Adjust salt and pepper to taste.
6. Chill the Quinoa and Black-Eyed Pea Salad in the refrigerator for at least 30 minutes to let the flavors meld.
7. Before serving, toss the salad again and adjust the seasoning if necessary.

Zoodle (Zucchini Noodle) Primavera with Grilled Chicken

2 servings | 25 minutes

Cal 350
Fat 15 g
Carb 20 g
Protein 30 g
Sodium 350 mg
Potassium 450 mg
Phosphorus 200 mg

INGREDIENTS

For Grilled Chicken:
- 4 boneless, skinless chicken breasts
- 2 tablespoons olive oil
- 1 teaspoon dried Italian seasoning
- Salt and pepper to taste

For Zoodle Primavera:
- 4 medium zucchinis, spiralized into noodles (zoodles)
- 1 cup cherry tomatoes, halved
- 1 bell pepper, thinly sliced
- 1 cup broccoli florets
- 1 carrot, julienned
- 2 cloves garlic, minced
- 2 tablespoons olive oil
- 1/2 cup grated Parmesan cheese
- Fresh basil for garnish (optional)

DIRECTIONS

For Grilled Chicken:
1. Preheat the grill or grill pan over medium-high heat.
2. In a bowl, mix olive oil, dried Italian seasoning, salt, and pepper.
3. Rub the chicken breasts with the prepared seasoning mixture.
4. Grill the chicken breasts for 6-7 minutes per side or until they reach an internal temperature of 165°F (74°C).
5. Allow the chicken to rest for a few minutes before slicing.

For Zoodle Primavera:
6. In a large skillet, heat olive oil over medium heat.
7. Add minced garlic and sauté for 1 minute until fragrant.
8. Add cherry tomatoes, bell pepper, broccoli, and julienned carrot to the skillet. Cook for 5-7 minutes until the vegetables are tender-crisp.
9. Add the zucchini noodles (zoodles) to the skillet and toss for 2-3 minutes until they are just tender.
10. Sprinkle-grated Parmesan cheese over the zoodles and vegetables. Toss until the cheese is melted and everything is well combined.
11. Serve the Zoodle Primavera in bowls, topped with sliced grilled chicken.
12. Garnish with fresh basil if desired.

Low-Sodium Minestrone Soup with Whole Wheat Bread

2 servings | 40 minutes

Cal 250
Fat 5 g
Carb 45 g
Protein 10 g
Sodium 200 mg
Potassium 400 mg
Phosphorus 150 mg

INGREDIENTS

For Minestrone Soup:
- 2 tablespoons olive oil
- 1 onion, finely chopped
- 2 cloves garlic, minced
- 2 carrots, diced
- 2 celery stalks, diced
- 1 zucchini, diced
- 1 cup green beans, cut into bite-sized pieces
- 1 can (14 ounces) low-sodium diced tomatoes
- 1 can (14 ounces) low-sodium kidney beans, drained and rinsed
- 1/2 cup whole wheat pasta (small shapes like shells or elbows)
- 4 cups low-sodium vegetable broth
- 2 teaspoons dried Italian herbs (basil, oregano, thyme)
- Salt and pepper to taste
- Fresh parsley for garnish (optional)

For Whole Wheat Bread:
- 4 slices whole wheat bread
- Olive oil for brushing (optional)

DIRECTIONS

For Minestrone Soup:
1. In a large pot, heat olive oil over medium heat. Add chopped onion and minced garlic. Sauté for 2-3 minutes until fragrant.
2. Add diced carrots, celery, zucchini, and green beans to the pot. Cook for an additional 5-7 minutes until the vegetables begin to soften.
3. Pour in the low-sodium vegetable broth and add the diced tomatoes, kidney beans, whole wheat pasta, and dried Italian herbs.
4. Bring the soup to a boil, then reduce the heat to low, cover, and simmer for 15-20 minutes or until the vegetables and pasta are tender.
5. Season the soup with salt and pepper to taste.
6. Garnish with fresh parsley if desired.

For Whole Wheat Bread:
1. Preheat the oven to 350°F (175°C).
2. Place the whole wheat bread slices on a baking sheet.
3. Optionally, brush each slice with a little olive oil for added flavor.
4. Bake in the preheated oven for 8-10 minutes or until the bread is toasted and crisp.

Serve the Low-Sodium Minestrone Soup with a side of Whole Wheat Bread.

Baked Sweet Potato with Kidney Beans and Salsa

2 servings | 60 minutes

Cal 300
Fat 1 g
Carb 65 g
Protein 10 g
Sodium 300 mg
Potassium 600 mg
Phosphorus 150 mg

INGREDIENTS

- 4 medium-sized sweet potatoes
- 1 can (15 ounces) kidney beans, drained and rinsed
- 1 cup corn kernels (fresh or frozen)
- 1 cup cherry tomatoes, diced
- 1/2 red onion, finely chopped
- 1 jalapeño, seeds removed and finely chopped
- 1/4 cup fresh cilantro, chopped
- Juice of 1 lime
- Salt and pepper to taste
- Greek yogurt for topping (optional)

DIRECTIONS

1. Preheat the oven to 400°F (200°C).
2. Wash sweet potatoes and prick them several times with a fork. Place them on a baking sheet.
3. Bake sweet potatoes in the preheated oven for 45-60 minutes or until they are tender when pierced with a fork.
4. While the sweet potatoes are baking, prepare the salsa. In a bowl, combine kidney beans, corn kernels, diced cherry tomatoes, finely chopped red onion, chopped jalapeño, cilantro, lime juice, salt, and pepper. Mix well.
5. Once the sweet potatoes are baked, let them cool slightly.
6. Slice each sweet potato lengthwise and fluff the insides with a fork.
7. Spoon the kidney bean and corn salsa generously over each sweet potato.
8. Optionally, top with a dollop of Greek yogurt for added creaminess.

Sesame Ginger Tofu Stir-Fry with Brown Rice

2 servings | 30 minutes

Cal 400
Fat 15 g
Carb 55 g
Protein 15 g
Sodium 350 mg
Potassium 500 mg
Phosphorus 200 mg

INGREDIENTS

For Sesame Ginger Tofu:
- 1 block (14 ounces) extra-firm tofu, pressed and cubed
- 2 tablespoons soy sauce (low-sodium)
- 1 tablespoon sesame oil
- 1 tablespoon rice vinegar
- 1 tablespoon maple syrup or agave nectar
- 1 tablespoon fresh ginger, grated
- 2 cloves garlic, minced
- 1 tablespoon sesame seeds

For Stir-Fry:
- 2 cups broccoli florets
- 1 bell pepper, thinly sliced
- 1 carrot, julienned
- 1 cup snap peas, ends trimmed
- 1 tablespoon vegetable oil
- 3 cups cooked brown rice

DIRECTIONS

For Sesame Ginger Tofu:
1. In a bowl, whisk together soy sauce, sesame oil, rice vinegar, maple syrup (or agave nectar), grated ginger, and minced garlic.
2. Add cubed tofu to the marinade, gently toss to coat, and let it marinate for at least 15 minutes.
3. Heat a skillet over medium-high heat. Add marinated tofu, including the marinade, and cook for 5-7 minutes or until the tofu is golden and has absorbed the flavors.
4. Sprinkle sesame seeds over the tofu and cook for an additional 2 minutes. Set aside.

For Stir-Fry:
5. In the same skillet, add vegetable oil over medium-high heat.
6. Add broccoli, bell pepper, julienned carrot, and snap peas. Stir-fry for 5-7 minutes until the vegetables are tender-crisp.
7. Add the cooked sesame ginger tofu to the skillet and toss to combine with the vegetables.
8. Serve the sesame ginger tofu and vegetable stir-fry over cooked brown rice.

Lemon Garlic Shrimp Skewers with Quinoa

2 servings | 45 minutes

Cal 350
Fat 10 g
Carb 35 g
Protein 30 g
Sodium 350 mg
Potassium 300 mg
Phosphorus 200 mg

INGREDIENTS

For Lemon Garlic Shrimp Skewers:
- 1 pound large shrimp, peeled and deveined
- Zest and juice of 1 lemon
- 3 cloves garlic, minced
- 2 tablespoons olive oil
- 1 teaspoon dried oregano
- Salt and pepper to taste
- Wooden skewers, soaked in water for 30 minutes

For Quinoa:
- 1 cup quinoa, rinsed
- 2 cups water or low-sodium vegetable broth
- 1 tablespoon olive oil
- Salt to taste

For Serving:
- Fresh parsley for garnish
- Lemon wedges

DIRECTIONS

For Lemon Garlic Shrimp Skewers:
1. In a bowl, combine lemon zest, lemon juice, minced garlic, olive oil, dried oregano, salt, and pepper.
2. Add peeled and deveined shrimp to the marinade. Toss to coat the shrimp evenly. Let it marinate for at least 15 minutes.
3. Preheat the grill or grill pan over medium-high heat.
4. Thread the marinated shrimp onto the soaked wooden skewers.
5. Grill the shrimp skewers for 2-3 minutes per side or until they turn pink and opaque.

For Quinoa:
1. In a medium saucepan, combine quinoa, water (or vegetable broth), olive oil, and a pinch of salt.
2. Bring the mixture to a boil, then reduce the heat to low, cover, and simmer for 15 minutes or until the quinoa is cooked and water is absorbed.
3. Fluff the quinoa with a fork.

Serve Lemon Garlic Shrimp Skewers over a bed of cooked quinoa.

For Serving:
1. Garnish with fresh parsley and serve with lemon wedges on the side.
2. Optionally, drizzle extra olive oil over the dish for added richness.

Chicken and Vegetable Brown Rice Bowl

2 servings | 45 minutes

Cal 400
Fat 10 g
Carb 55 g
Protein 25 g
Sodium 350 mg
Potassium 400 mg
Phosphorus 250 mg

INGREDIENTS

For Chicken Marinade:
- 1 pound boneless, skinless chicken breasts, thinly sliced
- 2 tablespoons soy sauce (low-sodium)
- 1 tablespoon sesame oil
- 1 tablespoon rice vinegar
- 1 tablespoon honey or maple syrup
- 2 cloves garlic, minced
- 1 teaspoon fresh ginger, grated

For Stir-Fried Vegetables:
- 2 tablespoons vegetable oil
- 1 bell pepper, thinly sliced
- 1 carrot, julienned
- 1 zucchini, sliced
- 1 cup broccoli florets
- 2 green onions, sliced
- Sesame seeds for garnish (optional)

For Brown Rice:
- 2 cups cooked brown rice

DIRECTIONS

For Chicken Marinade:
1. In a bowl, whisk together soy sauce, sesame oil, rice vinegar, honey (or maple syrup), minced garlic, and grated ginger.
2. Add thinly sliced chicken to the marinade, ensuring it is well-coated. Let it marinate for at least 15 minutes.
3. In a large skillet or wok, heat a small amount of vegetable oil over medium-high heat.
4. Add the marinated chicken and stir-fry for 5-7 minutes or until cooked through and lightly browned. Set aside.

For Stir-Fried Vegetables:
1. In the same skillet, add additional vegetable oil if needed.
2. Add sliced bell pepper, julienned carrot, sliced zucchini, broccoli florets, and green onions. Stir-fry for 5-7 minutes until the vegetables are tender-crisp.

For Brown Rice:
1. Prepare brown rice according to package instructions.
2. Fluff the cooked rice with a fork.

Assembling Chicken and Vegetable Brown Rice Bowl:
1. Divide the cooked brown rice among serving bowls.
2. Top the rice with the stir-fried vegetables and the cooked, marinated chicken.
3. Garnish with sesame seeds if desired.

Cabbage and White Bean Stew

2 servings — **35 minutes**

Cal 250
Fat 5 g
Carb 40 g
Protein 12 g
Sodium 350 mg
Potassium 500 mg
Phosphorus 150 mg

INGREDIENTS

- 1 tablespoon olive oil
- 1 onion, finely chopped
- 2 cloves garlic, minced
- 1 small head of cabbage, shredded
- 2 carrots, peeled and sliced
- 1 can (15 ounces) white beans, drained and rinsed
- 1 can (14 ounces) diced tomatoes (low-sodium)
- 4 cups vegetable broth (low-sodium)
- 1 teaspoon dried thyme
- 1 teaspoon paprika
- Salt and pepper to taste
- Fresh parsley for garnish (optional)

DIRECTIONS

1. In a large pot, heat olive oil over medium heat.
2. Add finely chopped onion and minced garlic. Sauté for 3-5 minutes until the onion is translucent.
3. Add sliced carrots and shredded cabbage to the pot. Cook for an additional 5 minutes, stirring occasionally.
4. Pour in vegetable broth, diced tomatoes, and drained white beans. Stir well.
5. Season the stew with dried thyme, paprika, salt, and pepper. Adjust the seasoning according to taste.
6. Bring the stew to a boil, then reduce the heat to low, cover, and simmer for 20-25 minutes or until the vegetables are tender.
7. Check the seasoning and adjust if necessary.
8. Serve the Cabbage and White Bean Stew hot, garnished with fresh parsley if desired.

Vegetarian Stuffed Bell Peppers with Lentils

2 servings | 65 minutes

Cal 300
Fat 5 g
Carb 50 g
Protein 15 g
Sodium 300 mg
Potassium 400 mg
Phosphorus 200 mg

INGREDIENTS

- 4 large bell peppers, halved and seeds removed
- 1 cup dry green or brown lentils, rinsed
- 2 cups vegetable broth (low-sodium)
- 1 tablespoon olive oil
- 1 onion, finely chopped
- 2 cloves garlic, minced
- 1 carrot, diced
- 1 zucchini, diced
- 1 can (14 ounces) diced tomatoes (low-sodium)
- 1 teaspoon dried oregano
- 1 teaspoon cumin
- Salt and pepper to taste
- 1 cup cooked brown rice
- 1 cup shredded mozzarella cheese (optional)

DIRECTIONS

1. Preheat the oven to 375°F (190°C).
2. In a medium saucepan, combine lentils and vegetable broth. Bring to a boil, then reduce heat to low, cover, and simmer for 25-30 minutes or until lentils are tender and most of the liquid is absorbed.
3. In a large skillet, heat olive oil over medium heat. Add chopped onion and minced garlic. Sauté for 3-5 minutes until the onion is translucent.
4. Add diced carrot and zucchini to the skillet. Cook for an additional 5 minutes until the vegetables are tender.
5. Stir in diced tomatoes, dried oregano, cumin, salt, and pepper. Cook for 5 more minutes.
6. Combine the cooked lentils and brown rice with the vegetable mixture. Mix well.
7. Place the bell pepper halves in a baking dish. Fill each half with the lentil and vegetable mixture.
8. If desired, sprinkle shredded mozzarella cheese on top of each stuffed pepper.
9. Cover the baking dish with aluminum foil and bake in the preheated oven for 25-30 minutes or until the peppers are tender.
10. Remove the foil and bake for an additional 5 minutes to melt the cheese (if used).
11. Serve the Vegetarian Stuffed Bell Peppers hot, optionally garnished with fresh herbs.

Turkey and Quinoa Stuffed Acorn Squash

2 servings | 65 minutes

Cal 400
Fat 15 g
Carb 45 g
Protein 25 g
Sodium 350 mg
Potassium 500 mg
Phosphorus 250 mg

INGREDIENTS

- 2 acorn squash, halved and seeds removed
- 1 cup quinoa, rinsed
- 2 cups water or low-sodium vegetable broth
- 1 tablespoon olive oil
- 1 onion, finely chopped
- 2 cloves garlic, minced
- 1 pound ground turkey
- 1 teaspoon ground cumin
- 1 teaspoon ground coriander
- 1 teaspoon smoked paprika
- Salt and pepper to taste
- 1/2 cup dried cranberries
- 1/4 cup chopped fresh parsley
- 1/4 cup crumbled feta cheese (optional)

DIRECTIONS

1. Preheat the oven to 375°F (190°C).
2. Place the acorn squash halves on a baking sheet, cut side down. Bake for 30-35 minutes or until the squash is fork-tender.
3. In a medium saucepan, combine quinoa and water (or vegetable broth). Bring to a boil, then reduce heat to low, cover, and simmer for 15-20 minutes or until the quinoa is cooked and liquid is absorbed.
4. In a large skillet, heat olive oil over medium heat. Add chopped onion and minced garlic. Sauté for 3-5 minutes until the onion is translucent.
5. Add ground turkey to the skillet and cook until browned.
6. Season the turkey with ground cumin, ground coriander, smoked paprika, salt, and pepper. Stir to combine.
7. Once the turkey is cooked through, add cooked quinoa, dried cranberries, and chopped fresh parsley to the skillet. Mix well.
8. Remove the acorn squash halves from the oven and turn them cut side up.
9. Fill each acorn squash half with the turkey and quinoa mixture.
10. Optionally, sprinkle crumbled feta cheese over each stuffed squash.
11. Return the stuffed acorn squash to the oven and bake for an additional 10-15 minutes or until the cheese is melted and the filling is heated through.
12. Serve the Turkey and Quinoa Stuffed Acorn Squash hot, optionally garnished with additional parsley.

Shrimp and Broccoli Alfredo with Whole Wheat Pasta

2 servings | 25 minutes

Cal 450
Fat 15 g
Carb 55 g
Protein 25 g

Sodium 350 mg
Potassium 400 mg
Phosphorus 200 mg

INGREDIENTS

- 8 ounces whole wheat fettuccine pasta
- 1 pound shrimp, peeled and deveined
- 2 tablespoons olive oil
- 3 cloves garlic, minced
- 2 cups broccoli florets
- 1 cup cherry tomatoes, halved
- 1 cup low-fat milk
- 1 cup grated Parmesan cheese
- 2 tablespoons cream cheese
- Salt and pepper to taste
- Red pepper flakes for optional heat
- Fresh basil for garnish (optional)

DIRECTIONS

1. Cook the whole wheat fettuccine pasta according to package instructions. Drain and set aside.
2. In a large skillet, heat olive oil over medium heat. Add minced garlic and sauté for 1 minute until fragrant.
3. Add shrimp to the skillet and cook for 2-3 minutes per side or until they are pink and opaque. Remove the shrimp from the skillet and set aside.
4. In the same skillet, add broccoli florets and cherry tomatoes. Sauté for 3-5 minutes until the vegetables are tender-crisp.
5. Lower the heat to medium-low. Pour in low-fat milk, grated Parmesan cheese, and cream cheese. Stir continuously until the cheese is melted and the sauce is smooth.
6. Season the sauce with salt, pepper, and red pepper flakes to taste.
7. Add the cooked shrimp back to the skillet and stir to coat them with the Alfredo sauce.
8. Toss the cooked whole wheat fettuccine pasta into the skillet and mix until everything is well combined.
9. Serve the Shrimp and Broccoli Alfredo over whole wheat pasta hot, garnished with fresh basil if desired.

Grilled Eggplant and Mozzarella Sandwich on Whole Grain Bread

2 servings | 20 minutes

Cal 350
Fat 15 g
Carb 40 g
Protein 15 g

Sodium 350 mg
Potassium 450 mg
Phosphorus 200 mg

INGREDIENTS

- 1 medium-sized eggplant, sliced
- 2 tablespoons olive oil
- Salt and pepper to taste
- 4 slices whole grain bread
- 4 ounces fresh mozzarella cheese, sliced
- 1 large tomato, sliced
- Fresh basil leaves
- Balsamic glaze for drizzling (optional)

DIRECTIONS

1. Preheat the grill or grill pan over medium-high heat.
2. Brush eggplant slices with olive oil and season with salt and pepper.
3. Grill the eggplant slices for 2-3 minutes per side or until they are tender and have grill marks. Set aside.
4. Toast the whole grain bread slices on the grill for 1-2 minutes on each side.
5. Assemble the sandwiches by layering grilled eggplant slices, fresh mozzarella cheese, tomato slices, and fresh basil leaves between the slices of whole grain bread.
6. Drizzle with balsamic glaze if desired.
7. Optional: Heat the assembled sandwiches on the grill for an additional 1-2 minutes per side to melt the mozzarella cheese.
8. Serve the Grilled Eggplant and Mozzarella Sandwiches hot.

Asian-Inspired Beef and Broccoli Stir-Fry with Cauliflower Rice

2 servings | 30 minutes

Cal 400
Fat 15 g
Carb 35 g
Protein 30 g
Sodium 500 mg
Potassium 600 mg
Phosphorus 250 mg

INGREDIENTS

For Beef Marinade:
- 1 pound flank steak, thinly sliced
- 2 tablespoons soy sauce (low-sodium)
- 1 tablespoon oyster sauce
- 1 tablespoon hoisin sauce
- 1 tablespoon sesame oil
- 1 tablespoon rice vinegar
- 2 teaspoons cornstarch
- 1 teaspoon fresh ginger, grated
- 2 cloves garlic, minced

For Stir-Fry:
- 2 tablespoons vegetable oil
- 4 cups broccoli florets
- 1 red bell pepper, thinly sliced
- 1 carrot, julienned
- 1 cup snap peas, ends trimmed

For Cauliflower Rice:
- 1 medium-sized cauliflower, grated
- 1 tablespoon sesame oil
- 2 green onions, sliced
- Sesame seeds for garnish
- Soy sauce for serving

DIRECTIONS

For Beef Marinade:
1. In a bowl, whisk together soy sauce, oyster sauce, hoisin sauce, sesame oil, rice vinegar, cornstarch, grated ginger, and minced garlic.
2. Add thinly sliced flank steak to the marinade. Toss to coat and let it marinate for at least 15 minutes.

For Stir-Fry:
3. Heat vegetable oil in a wok or large skillet over high heat.
4. Add marinated beef to the hot wok and stir-fry for 2-3 minutes or until the beef is browned and cooked through. Remove from the wok and set aside.
5. In the same wok, add a bit more oil if needed. Stir-fry broccoli, red bell pepper, julienned carrot, and snap peas for 5-7 minutes or until the vegetables are tender-crisp.

For Cauliflower Rice:
6. In a separate skillet, heat sesame oil over medium heat.
7. Add grated cauliflower to the skillet and stir-fry for 3-5 minutes or until the cauliflower is tender.
8. Stir in sliced green onions.

Assembling:
9. Serve the Asian-inspired beef and Broccoli Stir-Fry over a bed of cauliflower rice.
10. Garnish with sesame seeds and drizzle with soy sauce.

Chickpea Salad with Cucumber, Tomatoes, and Feta Cheese

2 servings | 45 minutes

Cal 300
Fat 12 g
Carb 15 g
Protein 12 g

Sodium 400 mg
Potassium 500 mg
Phosphorus 150 mg

INGREDIENTS

- 2 cans (15 ounces each) chickpeas, drained and rinsed
- 1 cucumber, diced
- 1 pint cherry tomatoes, halved
- 1/2 red onion, finely chopped
- 1/2 cup crumbled feta cheese
- 1/4 cup fresh parsley, chopped
- 1/4 cup extra-virgin olive oil
- 2 tablespoons red wine vinegar
- 1 teaspoon dried oregano
- Salt and pepper to taste
- Lemon wedges for serving (optional)

DIRECTIONS

1. In a large mixing bowl, combine chickpeas, diced cucumber, halved cherry tomatoes, finely chopped red onion, crumbled feta cheese, and chopped fresh parsley.
2. In a small bowl, whisk together extra-virgin olive oil, red wine vinegar, dried oregano, salt, and pepper to create the dressing.
3. Pour the dressing over the chickpea mixture and toss gently until all ingredients are well coated.
4. Adjust the seasoning to taste with additional salt and pepper if needed.
5. Let the salad marinate in the refrigerator for at least 30 minutes to allow the flavors to meld.
6. Before serving, toss the salad again and sprinkle additional fresh parsley on top.
7. Optionally, serve the Chickpea Salad with Lemon wedges on the side for a burst of citrus flavor.

Lemon Dill Salmon Patties with Steamed Green Beans

2 servings | 25 minutes

Cal 350
Fat 20 g
Carb 15 g
Protein 30 g

Sodium 400 mg
Potassium 500 mg
Phosphorus 250 mg

INGREDIENTS

For Salmon Patties:
- 2 cans (14.75 ounces each) pink salmon, drained and bones removed
- 1/2 cup breadcrumbs (whole wheat for added fiber)
- 2 eggs, beaten
- 1/4 cup mayonnaise
- Zest of 1 lemon
- 2 tablespoons fresh dill, chopped
- Salt and pepper to taste
- 2 tablespoons olive oil for cooking

For Steamed Green Beans:
- 2 cups fresh green beans, trimmed
- 1 tablespoon olive oil
- 1 tablespoon lemon juice
- Salt and pepper to taste

DIRECTIONS

For Salmon Patties:
1. In a large mixing bowl, combine drained salmon, breadcrumbs, beaten eggs, mayonnaise, lemon zest, chopped dill, salt, and pepper. Mix until well combined.
2. Divide the mixture into equal portions and shape them into patties.
3. Heat olive oil in a skillet over medium-high heat.
4. Cook the salmon patties for 3-4 minutes per side or until golden brown and cooked through.

For Steamed Green Beans:
5. Steam green beans until they are tender-crisp, about 4-5 minutes.
6. In a separate bowl, whisk together olive oil, lemon juice, salt, and pepper to create a simple dressing.
7. Toss the steamed green beans in the dressing until they are well coated.

Vegetarian Lentil and Spinach Curry with Basmati Rice

2 servings — **25 minutes**

Cal 350
Fat 10 g
Carb 50 g
Protein 15 g
Sodium 400 mg
Potassium 600 mg
Phosphorus 200 mg

INGREDIENTS

For Lentil and Spinach Curry:
- 1 cup dry green or brown lentils, rinsed
- 1 large onion, finely chopped
- 3 cloves garlic, minced
- 1 tablespoon ginger, grated
- 1 can (14 ounces) diced tomatoes (low-sodium)
- 1 can (14 ounces) coconut milk (light for lower fat)
- 1 teaspoon ground turmeric
- 1 teaspoon ground cumin
- 1 teaspoon ground coriander
- 1 teaspoon chili powder (adjust to taste)
- 1 teaspoon garam masala
- 4 cups fresh spinach, chopped
- 2 tablespoons vegetable oil
- Salt and pepper to taste
- Fresh cilantro for garnish

For Basmati Rice:
- 1 cup basmati rice
- 2 cups water
- 1/2 teaspoon salt

DIRECTIONS

For Basmati Rice:
1. Rinse basmati rice under cold water until the water runs clear.
2. In a saucepan, combine basmati rice, water, and salt.
3. Bring to a boil, then reduce heat to low, cover, and simmer for 15-20 minutes or until the rice is cooked and water is absorbed.

For Lentil and Spinach Curry:
1. In a large pot, heat vegetable oil over medium heat. Add chopped onion and sauté until translucent.
2. Add minced garlic and grated ginger to the pot. Sauté for an additional 2 minutes until fragrant.
3. Stir in ground turmeric, ground cumin, ground coriander, chili powder, and garam masala. Cook for 1-2 minutes to toast the spices.
4. Add rinsed lentils, diced tomatoes, and coconut milk to the pot. Season with salt and pepper. Bring to a simmer and let it cook for 20-25 minutes or until the lentils are tender.
5. Add chopped spinach to the pot and stir until wilted.
6. Adjust seasoning if needed and let the curry simmer for an additional 5 minutes.

Turkey and Vegetable Lettuce Wraps with Hummus

2 servings | 25 minutes

Cal 350
Fat 10 g
Carb 50 g
Protein 15 g
Sodium 400 mg
Potassium 600 mg
Phosphorus 200 mg

INGREDIENTS

For Turkey Filling:
- 1 pound lean ground turkey
- 1 tablespoon olive oil
- 1 onion, finely chopped
- 2 cloves garlic, minced
- 1 bell pepper, diced
- 1 zucchini, diced
- 1 carrot, shredded
- 1 teaspoon ground cumin
- 1 teaspoon ground coriander
- Salt and pepper to taste
- Fresh cilantro or parsley, chopped for garnish

For Lettuce Wraps:
- Large lettuce leaves (such as iceberg or butter lettuce)
- Hummus for spreading

DIRECTIONS

For Turkey Filling:
1. In a large skillet, heat olive oil over medium heat.
2. Add chopped onion and sauté until translucent.
3. Add minced garlic and sauté for an additional 1-2 minutes until fragrant.
4. Add ground turkey to the skillet and cook until browned, breaking it up with a spatula.
5. Stir in diced bell pepper, diced zucchini, and shredded carrot. Cook for 5-7 minutes until the vegetables are tender.
6. Season the mixture with ground cumin, ground coriander, salt, and pepper. Stir to combine.
7. Garnish with chopped fresh cilantro or parsley.

For Lettuce Wraps:
1. Spoon the turkey and vegetable filling onto large lettuce leaves.
2. Spread hummus on each lettuce leaf.
3. Fold the sides of the lettuce over the filling and roll to form a wrap.
4. Serve the Turkey and Vegetable Lettuce Wraps immediately.

Dinner

Baked Tilapia with Herbed Quinoa and Steamed Asparagus

2 servings | 20 minutes

Cal 400
Fat 15 g
Carb 35 g
Protein 30 g
Sodium 350 mg
Potassium 500 mg
Phosphorus 200 mg

INGREDIENTS

For Baked Tilapia:
- 4 tilapia fillets
- 2 tablespoons olive oil
- 1 lemon, sliced
- 2 teaspoons dried oregano
- 1 teaspoon garlic powder
- Salt and pepper to taste

For Herbed Quinoa:
- 1 cup quinoa, rinsed
- 2 cups low-sodium vegetable broth
- 1 tablespoon olive oil
- 1 teaspoon dried thyme
- 1 teaspoon dried rosemary
- Salt and pepper to taste

For Steamed Asparagus:
- 1 bunch asparagus, ends trimmed
- 1 tablespoon olive oil
- 1 teaspoon lemon zest
- Salt and pepper to taste

DIRECTIONS

For Baked Tilapia:
1. Preheat the oven to 400°F (200°C).
2. Place tilapia fillets on a baking sheet lined with parchment paper.
3. Drizzle olive oil over the fillets and rub with dried oregano, garlic powder, salt, and pepper.
4. Lay lemon slices on top of the fillets.
5. Bake in the preheated oven for 12-15 minutes or until the tilapia is cooked through and flakes easily with a fork.

For Herbed Quinoa:
6. In a medium saucepan, combine quinoa, low-sodium vegetable broth, olive oil, dried thyme, dried rosemary, salt, and pepper.
7. Bring the mixture to a boil, then reduce heat to low, cover, and simmer for 15-20 minutes or until the quinoa is cooked and liquid is absorbed.
8. Fluff the quinoa with a fork.

For Steamed Asparagus:
9. Steam asparagus in a steamer basket or microwave-safe dish for 3-5 minutes or until crisp-tender.
10. Drizzle olive oil over the steamed asparagus, sprinkle with lemon zest and season with salt and pepper.
11. Serve Baked Tilapia over a bed of Herbed Quinoa with Steamed Asparagus on the side.

Vegetarian Spinach and Chickpea Coconut Curry

2 servings | 30 minutes

Cal 350
Fat 15 g
Carb 40 g
Protein 12 g
Sodium 400 mg
Potassium 500 mg
Phosphorus 150 mg

INGREDIENTS

- 1 tablespoon coconut oil
- 1 large onion, finely chopped
- 3 cloves garlic, minced
- 1 tablespoon ginger, grated
- 1 tablespoon curry powder
- 1 teaspoon ground cumin
- 1 teaspoon ground coriander
- 1 teaspoon turmeric
- 1 can (14 ounces) chickpeas, drained and rinsed
- 1 can (14 ounces) diced tomatoes (low-sodium)
- 1 can (14 ounces) coconut milk (light for lower fat)
- 4 cups fresh spinach, chopped
- Salt and pepper to taste
- Fresh cilantro for garnish
- Cooked brown rice for serving

DIRECTIONS

1. In a large skillet or pot, heat coconut oil over medium heat.
2. Add chopped onion and sauté until translucent.
3. Stir in minced garlic and grated ginger. Sauté for an additional 2 minutes until fragrant.
4. Add curry powder, ground cumin, ground coriander, and turmeric. Cook for 1-2 minutes to toast the spices.
5. Add drained chickpeas, diced tomatoes, and coconut milk to the pot. Season with salt and pepper. Bring to a simmer and let it cook for 15-20 minutes.
6. Stir in chopped spinach and cook until wilted.
7. Adjust seasoning if needed. Simmer for an additional 5 minutes.
8. Serve the Vegetarian Spinach and Chickpea Coconut Curry over cooked brown rice.
9. Garnish with fresh cilantro.

Turkey and Vegetable Kabobs with Brown Rice

2 servings | 30 minutes

Cal 400
Fat 15 g
Carb 35 g
Protein 30 g
Sodium 350 mg
Potassium 450 mg
Phosphorus 250 mg

INGREDIENTS

For Turkey and Vegetable Kabobs:
- 1 pound turkey breast, cut into cubes
- 1 red bell pepper, cut into chunks
- 1 yellow bell pepper, cut into chunks
- 1 zucchini, sliced
- 1 red onion, cut into chunks
- 1 cup cherry tomatoes
- 2 tablespoons olive oil
- 1 tablespoon balsamic vinegar
- 1 teaspoon dried oregano
- 1 teaspoon garlic powder
- Salt and pepper to taste
- Wooden or metal skewers

For Brown Rice:
- 1 cup brown rice
- 2 cups water
- 1/2 teaspoon salt

DIRECTIONS

Turkey and Vegetable Kabobs:
1. If using wooden skewers, soak them in water for 30 minutes to prevent burning.
2. In a bowl, combine olive oil, balsamic vinegar, dried oregano, garlic powder, salt, and pepper.
3. Thread turkey cubes, bell peppers, zucchini slices, red onion chunks, and cherry tomatoes onto skewers.
4. Brush the skewers with the prepared marinade.
5. Preheat the grill or grill pan over medium-high heat.
6. Grill the kabobs for 10-15 minutes, turning occasionally, until the turkey is cooked through and the vegetables are tender.

For Brown Rice:
7. Rinse brown rice under cold water until the water runs clear.
8. In a saucepan, combine brown rice, water, and salt.
9. Bring to a boil, then reduce heat to low, cover, and simmer for 45-50 minutes or until the rice is cooked and water is absorbed.
10. Fluff the brown rice with a fork.
11. Serve Turkey and Vegetable Kabobs over a bed of Brown Rice.

Lemon Herb Chicken Thighs with Cauliflower Mash

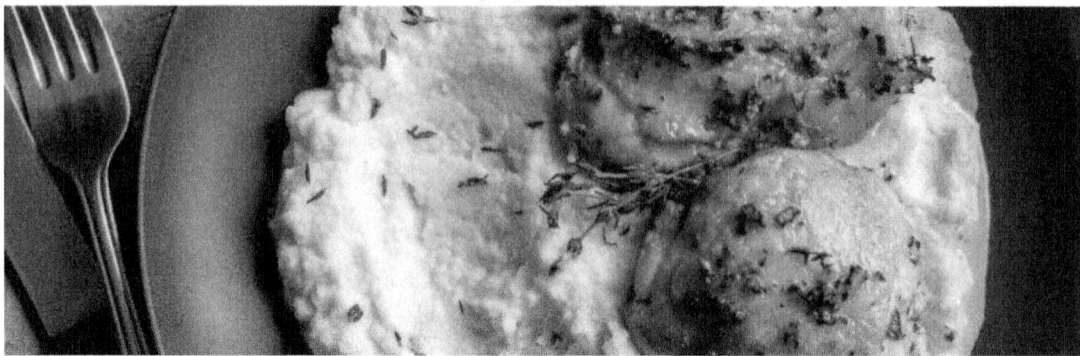

2 servings | 40 minutes

Cal 350
Fat 20 g
Carb 10 g
Protein 30 g
Sodium 400 mg
Potassium 600 mg
Phosphorus 250 mg

INGREDIENTS

For Lemon Herb Chicken Thighs:
- 4 bone-in, skin-on chicken thighs
- 2 tablespoons olive oil
- 1 lemon, juiced and zested
- 2 cloves garlic, minced
- 1 teaspoon dried thyme
- 1 teaspoon dried rosemary
- Salt and pepper to taste

For Cauliflower Mash:
- 1 large head cauliflower, cut into florets
- 2 tablespoons butter (or olive oil for a lighter option)
- 1/4 cup grated Parmesan cheese
- Salt and pepper to taste
- Fresh parsley for garnish

DIRECTIONS

For Lemon Herb Chicken Thighs:
1. Preheat the oven to 400°F (200°C).
2. In a small bowl, mix together olive oil, lemon juice, lemon zest, minced garlic, dried thyme, dried rosemary, salt, and pepper.
3. Place chicken thighs in a baking dish. Brush the chicken thighs with the lemon herb mixture, ensuring they are well coated.
4. Bake in the preheated oven for 30-35 minutes or until the chicken is golden brown and cooked through.

For Cauliflower Mash:
5. Steam cauliflower florets until very tender, about 10-15 minutes.
6. Transfer steamed cauliflower to a food processor.
7. Add butter (or olive oil), grated Parmesan cheese, salt, and pepper.
8. Blend until smooth and creamy.

Salmon and Zucchini Noodle Stir-Fry

2 servings | 40 minutes

Cal 400
Fat 20 g
Carb 25 g
Protein 30 g
Sodium 400 mg
Potassium 600 mg
Phosphorus 250 mg

INGREDIENTS

For Salmon:
- 4 salmon fillets
- 2 tablespoons soy sauce (low-sodium)
- 1 tablespoon honey or maple syrup
- 1 tablespoon sesame oil
- 2 cloves garlic, minced
- 1 teaspoon ginger, grated
- 1 tablespoon olive oil for cooking

For Zucchini Noodle Stir-Fry:
- 4 medium zucchinis, spiralized into noodles
- 1 carrot, julienned
- 1 red bell pepper, thinly sliced
- 1 cup snap peas, ends trimmed
- 2 tablespoons soy sauce (low-sodium)
- 1 tablespoon oyster sauce
- 1 tablespoon sesame oil
- 2 green onions, sliced
- Sesame seeds for garnish (optional)

DIRECTIONS

For Salmon:
1. In a bowl, whisk together soy sauce, honey or maple syrup, sesame oil, minced garlic, and grated ginger.
2. Place salmon fillets in a shallow dish and pour half of the marinade over them. Let it marinate for at least 15 minutes.
3. In a skillet, heat olive oil over medium-high heat. Add marinated salmon fillets and cook for 4-5 minutes per side or until cooked through.
4. Pour the remaining marinade over the salmon during the last minute of cooking.

For Zucchini Noodle Stir-Fry:
5. In the same skillet, add a bit more oil if needed. Stir-fry spiralized zucchini, julienned carrot, sliced red bell pepper, and snap peas for 3-5 minutes or until vegetables are tender-crisp.
6. In a small bowl, whisk together soy sauce, oyster sauce, and sesame oil.
7. Pour the sauce over the vegetable mixture and toss to combine.
8. Add sliced green onions and cook for an additional 2 minutes.

Spaghetti Squash with Tomato and Basil Sauce

2 servings | 40 minutes

Cal 150
Fat 5 g
Carb 30 g
Protein 3 g
Sodium 300 mg
Potassium 400 mg
Phosphorus 100 mg

INGREDIENTS

For Spaghetti Squash:
- 1 medium-sized spaghetti squash
- 1 tablespoon olive oil
- Salt and pepper to taste

For Tomato and Basil Sauce:
- 2 tablespoons olive oil
- 3 cloves garlic, minced
- 1 can (28 ounces) crushed tomatoes
- 1 teaspoon dried oregano
- 1 teaspoon dried basil
- Salt and pepper to taste
- Fresh basil leaves for garnish
- Grated Parmesan cheese for serving (optional)

DIRECTIONS

For Spaghetti Squash:
1. Preheat the oven to 400°F (200°C).
2. Cut the spaghetti squash in half lengthwise and scoop out the seeds.
3. Drizzle the cut sides of the squash with olive oil and sprinkle with salt and pepper.
4. Place the squash, cut side down, on a baking sheet lined with parchment paper.
5. Bake in the preheated oven for 40-45 minutes or until the squash is tender and easily pierced with a fork.
6. Use a fork to scrape the strands of spaghetti squash into a bowl.

For Tomato and Basil Sauce:
7. In a skillet, heat olive oil over medium heat. Add minced garlic and sauté for 1-2 minutes until fragrant.
8. Pour in crushed tomatoes and add dried oregano and dried basil. Season with salt and pepper to taste.
9. Simmer the sauce for 15-20 minutes, stirring occasionally.
10. Adjust seasoning if needed and stir in fresh basil leaves.

Serve Spaghetti Squash topped with Tomato and Basil Sauce.

Miso-Glazed Cod with Stir-Fried Bok Choy

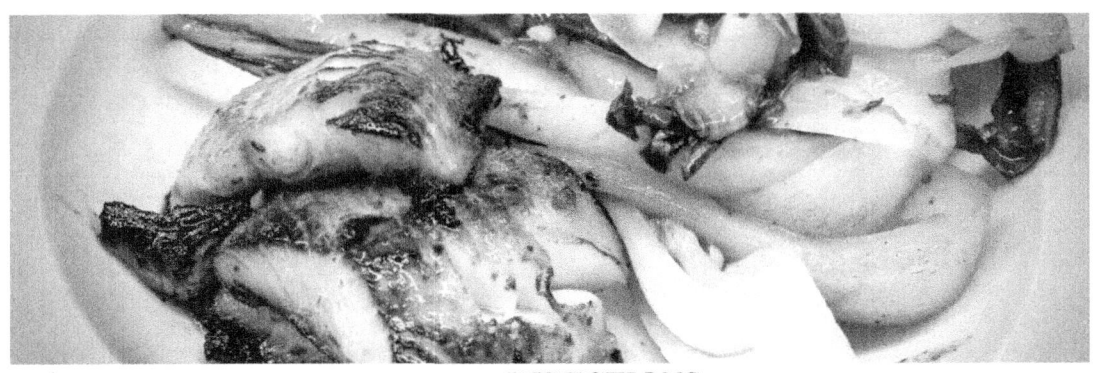

2 servings   40 minutes

Cal 150
Fat 5 g
Carb 30 g
Protein 3 g

Sodium 300 mg
Potassium 400 mg
Phosphorus 100 mg

INGREDIENTS

For Miso-Glazed Cod:
- 4 cod fillets
- 2 tablespoons white miso paste
- 1 tablespoon soy sauce (low-sodium)
- 1 tablespoon rice vinegar
- 1 tablespoon honey or maple syrup
- 1 teaspoon sesame oil
- 1 teaspoon ginger, grated
- 2 cloves garlic, minced
- Sesame seeds for garnish

For Stir-Fried Bok Choy:
- 4 baby bok choy, halved
- 1 tablespoon vegetable oil
- 2 teaspoons soy sauce (low-sodium)
- 1 teaspoon sesame oil
- 1 teaspoon ginger, grated
- 1 clove garlic, minced

DIRECTIONS

For Miso-Glazed Cod:
1. Preheat the oven to 400°F (200°C).
2. In a bowl, whisk together white miso paste, soy sauce, rice vinegar, honey or maple syrup, sesame oil, grated ginger, and minced garlic.
3. Place cod fillets on a baking sheet lined with parchment paper.
4. Brush the miso glaze over the cod fillets, ensuring they are well coated.
5. Bake in the preheated oven for 12-15 minutes or until the cod is cooked through and flakes easily with a fork.
6. Garnish with sesame seeds.

For Stir-Fried Bok Choy:
1. Heat vegetable oil in a wok or skillet over medium-high heat.
2. Add halved baby bok choy, grated ginger, and minced garlic. Stir-fry for 3-4 minutes until the bok choy is slightly wilted.
3. Drizzle soy sauce and sesame oil over the bok choy. Toss to combine.

Vegetarian Stuffed Portobello Mushrooms with Quinoa

2 servings | 30 minutes

Cal 300
Fat 15 g
Carb 30 g
Protein 12 g

Sodium 400 mg
Potassium 500 mg
Phosphorus 150 mg

INGREDIENTS

- 4 large Portobello mushrooms, stems removed
- 1 cup quinoa, cooked
- 1 tablespoon olive oil
- 1 onion, finely chopped
- 2 cloves garlic, minced
- 1 bell pepper, diced
- 1 zucchini, diced
- 1 carrot, shredded
- 1 cup cherry tomatoes, halved
- 1 cup fresh spinach, chopped
- 1 teaspoon dried oregano
- 1 teaspoon dried basil
- Salt and pepper to taste
- 1/2 cup feta cheese, crumbled (optional)
- Fresh parsley for garnish

DIRECTIONS

1. Preheat the oven to 375°F (190°C).
2. Clean the Portobello mushrooms and remove the stems. Place them on a baking sheet.
3. In a skillet, heat olive oil over medium heat. Add chopped onion and sauté until translucent.
4. Add minced garlic, diced bell pepper, diced zucchini, shredded carrot, cherry tomatoes, and chopped spinach to the skillet. Cook for 5-7 minutes until the vegetables are tender.
5. Stir in cooked quinoa, dried oregano, dried basil, salt, and pepper. Cook for an additional 2-3 minutes to let the flavors meld.
6. Spoon the quinoa and vegetable mixture into the Portobello mushrooms, pressing it down gently.
7. If using, sprinkle crumbled feta cheese over the stuffed mushrooms.
8. Bake in the preheated oven for 20-25 minutes or until the mushrooms are cooked and the filling is heated through.
9. Garnish with fresh parsley before serving.

Grilled Shrimp Salad with Avocado and Mango

2 servings | 15 minutes

Cal 300
Fat 15 g
Carb 25 g
Protein 20 g
Sodium 350 mg
Potassium 500 mg
Phosphorus 200 mg

INGREDIENTS

For Grilled Shrimp:
- 1 pound large shrimp, peeled and deveined
- 2 tablespoons olive oil
- 1 teaspoon smoked paprika
- 1 teaspoon garlic powder
- Salt and pepper to taste
- Wooden or metal skewers

For Salad:
- 6 cups mixed salad greens
- 1 avocado, sliced
- 1 mango, peeled and diced
- 1/4 cup red onion, thinly sliced
- 1/4 cup fresh cilantro, chopped

For Dressing:
- 2 tablespoons olive oil
- 2 tablespoons lime juice
- 1 tablespoon honey or maple syrup
- Salt and pepper to taste

DIRECTIONS

For Grilled Shrimp:
1. In a bowl, combine olive oil, smoked paprika, garlic powder, salt, and pepper.
2. Thread shrimp onto skewers and brush them with the olive oil mixture.
3. Preheat the grill or grill pan over medium-high heat.
4. Grill shrimp for 2-3 minutes per side or until they are opaque and cooked through.

For Salad:
5. In a large salad bowl, combine mixed salad greens, sliced avocado, diced mango, thinly sliced red onion, and chopped cilantro.

For Dressing:
6. In a small bowl, whisk together olive oil, lime juice, honey or maple syrup, salt, and pepper.

Assemble the Grilled Shrimp Salad:
7. Remove shrimp from skewers and place them on top of the salad.
8. Drizzle the dressing over the salad and toss gently to combine.
9. Serve immediately.

Chicken and Vegetable Korma with Basmati Rice

2 servings | 40 minutes

Cal 400
Fat 15 g
Carb 40 g
Protein 25 g
Sodium 400 mg
Potassium 500 mg
Phosphorus 250 mg

INGREDIENTS

For Chicken and Vegetable Korma:
- 1 pound boneless, skinless chicken breasts, cut into bite-sized pieces
- 1 cup carrots, sliced
- 1 cup green beans, chopped
- 1 onion, finely chopped
- 2 cloves garlic, minced
- 1 tablespoon ginger, grated
- 1/2 cup plain yogurt
- 1/2 cup coconut milk (light for lower fat)
- 2 tablespoons vegetable oil
- 2 tablespoons korma curry paste
- 1 teaspoon ground turmeric
- 1 teaspoon ground cumin
- 1 teaspoon ground coriander
- Salt and pepper to taste
- Fresh cilantro for garnish

For Basmati Rice:
- 1 cup basmati rice
- 2 cups water
- 1/2 teaspoon salt

DIRECTIONS

For Basmati Rice:
1. Rinse basmati rice under cold water until the water runs clear.
2. In a saucepan, combine basmati rice, water, and salt.
3. Bring to a boil, then reduce heat to low, cover, and simmer for 15-20 minutes or until the rice is cooked and water is absorbed.
4. Fluff the rice with a fork.

For Chicken and Vegetable Korma:
5. In a large skillet, heat vegetable oil over medium heat.
6. Add chopped onion and sauté until translucent.
7. Stir in minced garlic and grated ginger. Sauté for an additional 2 minutes until fragrant.
8. Add korma curry paste, ground turmeric, ground cumin, and ground coriander. Cook for 1-2 minutes to toast the spices.
9. Add chicken pieces to the skillet and cook until browned on all sides.
10. Add sliced carrots and chopped green beans to the skillet. Cook for 5-7 minutes until the vegetables are tender.
11. Stir in plain yogurt and coconut milk. Season with salt and pepper. Simmer for 10-15 minutes until the chicken is cooked through and the sauce thickens.
12. Adjust seasoning if needed.

Zesty Lime and Cilantro Chicken with Cabbage Slaw

2 servings | 40 minutes

Cal 300
Fat 15 g
Carb 20 g
Protein 25 g
Sodium 350 mg
Potassium 400 mg
Phosphorus 200 mg

INGREDIENTS

For Lime and Cilantro Chicken:
- 1 pound boneless, skinless chicken breasts, thinly sliced
- Zest and juice of 2 limes
- 3 tablespoons olive oil
- 2 tablespoons fresh cilantro, chopped
- 2 cloves garlic, minced
- 1 teaspoon ground cumin
- 1 teaspoon chili powder
- Salt and pepper to taste

For Cabbage Slaw:
- 4 cups green cabbage, thinly sliced
- 1 cup red cabbage, thinly sliced
- 1 carrot, julienned
- 1/2 red onion, thinly sliced
- 1/4 cup fresh cilantro, chopped
- 2 tablespoons apple cider vinegar
- 2 tablespoons olive oil
- 1 tablespoon honey or maple syrup
- Salt and pepper to taste

DIRECTIONS

For Lime and Cilantro Chicken:
1. In a bowl, combine lime zest, lime juice, olive oil, chopped cilantro, minced garlic, ground cumin, chili powder, salt, and pepper.
2. Add sliced chicken to the marinade, ensuring it is well coated. Let it marinate for at least 30 minutes.
3. Heat a skillet over medium-high heat. Cook the marinated chicken for 5-7 minutes or until fully cooked, stirring occasionally.

For Cabbage Slaw:
1. In a large bowl, combine green cabbage, red cabbage, julienned carrot, sliced red onion, and chopped cilantro.
2. In a small bowl, whisk together apple cider vinegar, olive oil, honey or maple syrup, salt, and pepper.
3. Pour the dressing over the cabbage mixture and toss to combine.

Egg Drop Soup with Shrimp and Vegetables

2 servings | **20 minutes**

Cal 150
Fat 5 g
Carb 10 g
Protein 15 g

Sodium 600 mg
Potassium 300 mg
Phosphorus 150 mg

INGREDIENTS

- 4 cups chicken or vegetable broth (low-sodium)
- 1/2 pound shrimp, peeled and deveined
- 1 cup mixed vegetables (carrots, peas, corn)
- 2 green onions, thinly sliced
- 2 tablespoons soy sauce (low-sodium)
- 1 tablespoon cornstarch
- 2 eggs, beaten
- 1 teaspoon sesame oil
- Salt and white pepper to taste
- Fresh cilantro for garnish (optional)

DIRECTIONS

1. In a pot, bring the chicken or vegetable broth to a gentle simmer.
2. Add shrimp and mixed vegetables to the simmering broth. Cook for 3-5 minutes or until the shrimp are pink and opaque.
3. In a small bowl, mix soy sauce and cornstarch to create a slurry.
4. Slowly pour the soy sauce and cornstarch slurry into the simmering soup while stirring continuously. Allow the soup to thicken slightly.
5. In a steady stream, pour the beaten eggs into the soup while stirring gently in one direction. This will create the characteristic egg ribbons.
6. Add sliced green onions and sesame oil to the soup. Season with salt and white pepper to taste.
7. Remove the soup from heat.

Mushroom and Spinach-Stuffed Chicken Breast with Green Beans

2 servings | 40 minutes

Cal 350
Fat 15 g
Carb 10 g
Protein 30 g
Sodium 400 mg
Potassium 500 mg
Phosphorus 250 mg

INGREDIENTS

For Mushroom and Spinach-Stuffed Chicken Breast:
- 4 boneless, skinless chicken breasts
- 1 cup mushrooms, finely chopped
- 2 cups fresh spinach, chopped
- 1/2 cup feta cheese, crumbled
- 2 cloves garlic, minced
- 1 tablespoon olive oil
- 1 teaspoon dried oregano
- 1 teaspoon dried thyme
- Salt and pepper to taste
- Toothpicks or kitchen twine

For Green Beans:
- 1 pound green beans, ends trimmed
- 2 tablespoons olive oil
- 1 tablespoon balsamic vinegar
- 1 teaspoon Dijon mustard
- Salt and pepper to taste

DIRECTIONS

For Mushroom and Spinach-Stuffed Chicken Breast:
1. Preheat the oven to 400°F (200°C).
2. In a skillet, heat olive oil over medium heat. Add minced garlic and sauté until fragrant.
3. Add chopped mushrooms to the skillet and cook until they release their moisture and become golden brown.
4. Stir in chopped spinach and cook until wilted. Remove from heat.
5. In a bowl, mix the mushroom and spinach mixture with crumbled feta, dried oregano, dried thyme, salt, and pepper.
6. Cut a pocket into each chicken breast. Stuff each pocket with the mushroom and spinach mixture, securing with toothpicks or kitchen twine.
7. Season the outside of the chicken breasts with salt and pepper.
8. Place the stuffed chicken breasts on a baking sheet lined with parchment paper. Bake in the preheated oven for 25-30 minutes or until the chicken is cooked through.

For Green Beans:
9. In a large bowl, whisk together olive oil, balsamic vinegar, Dijon mustard, salt, and pepper.
10. Add trimmed green beans to the bowl and toss until well coated.
11. Spread the green beans on a separate baking sheet.
12. Roast in the oven for 15-20 minutes or until the green beans are tender.

Quinoa and Black Bean Chili with Ground Turkey

2 servings | 35 minutes

Cal 400
Fat 15 g
Carb 40 g
Protein 25 g
Sodium 400 mg
Potassium 500 mg
Phosphorus 300 mg

INGREDIENTS

- 1 pound ground turkey
- 1 cup quinoa, uncooked
- 1 can (15 ounces) black beans, drained and rinsed
- 1 can (14 ounces) diced tomatoes (low-sodium)
- 1 bell pepper, diced
- 1 onion, diced
- 2 cloves garlic, minced
- 1 tablespoon chili powder
- 1 teaspoon ground cumin
- 1 teaspoon smoked paprika
- 1/2 teaspoon cayenne pepper (optional, for extra heat)
- Salt and pepper to taste
- 4 cups low-sodium chicken or vegetable broth
- Olive oil for cooking
- Optional toppings: shredded cheese, chopped green onions, cilantro, Greek yogurt

DIRECTIONS

1. Rinse quinoa under cold water.
2. In a large pot, heat olive oil over medium heat. Add diced onion, diced bell pepper, and minced garlic. Sauté until the vegetables are softened.
3. Add ground turkey to the pot and cook until browned.
4. Stir in chili powder, ground cumin, smoked paprika, cayenne pepper (if using), salt, and pepper. Cook for 1-2 minutes to toast the spices.
5. Add quinoa, black beans, diced tomatoes, and chicken or vegetable broth to the pot. Bring to a boil.
6. Reduce heat to low, cover, and simmer for 20-25 minutes or until the quinoa is cooked and the chili has thickened.
7. Adjust seasoning if needed.
8. Serve hot, topped with shredded cheese, chopped green onions, cilantro, and a dollop of Greek yogurt if desired.

Lemon Garlic Shrimp with Broccoli and Brown Rice

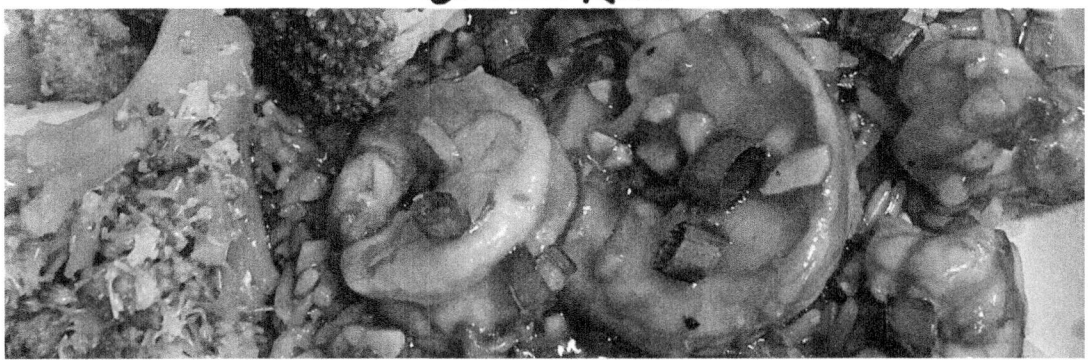

2 servings | 45 minutes

Cal 350
Fat 10 g
Carb 40 g
Protein 25 g
Sodium 350 mg
Potassium 400 mg
Phosphorus 250 mg

INGREDIENTS

For Lemon Garlic Shrimp:
- 1 pound large shrimp, peeled and deveined
- 3 tablespoons olive oil
- Zest and juice of 1 lemon
- 3 cloves garlic, minced
- 1 teaspoon dried oregano
- Salt and pepper to taste

For Broccoli and Brown Rice:
- 2 cups broccoli florets
- 1 cup brown rice, uncooked
- 4 cups water
- 1 tablespoon olive oil
- Salt to taste

DIRECTIONS

For Lemon Garlic Shrimp:
1. In a bowl, mix together olive oil, lemon zest, lemon juice, minced garlic, dried oregano, salt, and pepper.
2. Add peeled and deveined shrimp to the bowl, ensuring they are well coated. Let them marinate for at least 15 minutes.
3. In a skillet, heat olive oil over medium-high heat. Add marinated shrimp and cook for 2-3 minutes per side or until they are pink and opaque.

For Broccoli and Brown Rice:
4. In a saucepan, bring 4 cups of water to a boil. Add brown rice, reduce heat to low, cover, and simmer for 40-45 minutes or until the rice is cooked.
5. In the last 10 minutes of cooking, add broccoli florets to the simmering rice.
6. Drain any excess water and toss the cooked rice and broccoli with olive oil. Season with salt to taste.

Stuffed Bell Peppers with Ground Chicken and Brown Rice

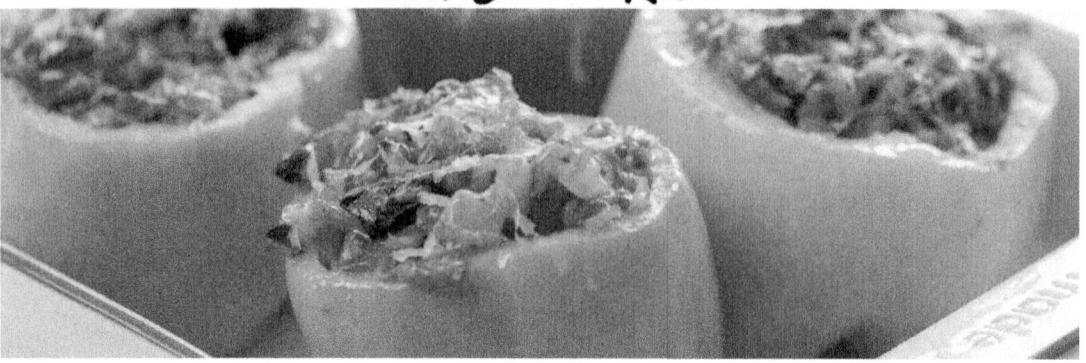

2 servings | 45 minutes

Cal 350
Fat 10 g
Carb 35 g
Protein 25 g
Sodium 400 mg
Potassium 500 mg
Phosphorus 200 mg

INGREDIENTS

- 4 large bell peppers, halved and seeds removed
- 1 pound ground chicken
- 1 cup brown rice, cooked
- 1 onion, finely chopped
- 2 cloves garlic, minced
- 1 can (15 ounces) black beans, drained and rinsed
- 1 cup corn kernels (fresh or frozen)
- 1 can (14 ounces) diced tomatoes, drained
- 1 teaspoon ground cumin
- 1 teaspoon chili powder
- 1/2 teaspoon smoked paprika
- Salt and pepper to taste
- 1 cup shredded cheese (cheddar or Monterey Jack)
- Fresh cilantro for garnish (optional)
- Olive oil for cooking

DIRECTIONS

1. Preheat the oven to 375°F (190°C).
2. Place halved bell peppers in a baking dish.
3. In a skillet, heat olive oil over medium heat. Add chopped onion and sauté until translucent.
4. Add minced garlic and ground chicken to the skillet. Cook until the chicken is browned.
5. Stir in cooked brown rice, black beans, corn kernels, diced tomatoes, ground cumin, chili powder, smoked paprika, salt, and pepper. Cook for an additional 5 minutes to let the flavors meld.
6. Spoon the chicken and rice mixture into the halved bell peppers.
7. Top each stuffed pepper with shredded cheese.
8. Cover the baking dish with foil and bake in the preheated oven for 25-30 minutes or until the peppers are tender.
9. Remove the foil and bake for an additional 5-10 minutes or until the cheese is melted and bubbly.

Chickpea and Tomato Curry with Cauliflower Rice

2 servings | **35 minutes**

Cal 300
Fat 15 g
Carb 35 g
Protein 10 g
Sodium 400 mg
Potassium 500 mg
Phosphorus 150 mg

INGREDIENTS

For Chickpea and Tomato Curry:
- 2 cans (15 ounces each) chickpeas, drained and rinsed
- 1 can (14 ounces) diced tomatoes
- 1 onion, finely chopped
- 2 cloves garlic, minced
- 1 tablespoon ginger, grated
- 1 tablespoon curry powder
- 1 teaspoon ground cumin
- 1 teaspoon ground coriander
- 1/2 teaspoon turmeric
- 1/2 teaspoon chili powder (adjust for spice preference)
- 1 can (14 ounces) coconut milk
- 2 tablespoons tomato paste
- 2 tablespoons olive oil
- Salt and pepper to taste
- Fresh cilantro for garnish

For Cauliflower Rice:
- 1 head cauliflower, grated or processed into rice-sized pieces
- 1 tablespoon olive oil
- Salt and pepper to taste

DIRECTIONS

For Chickpea and Tomato Curry:
1. In a large skillet, heat olive oil over medium heat. Add chopped onion and sauté until translucent.
2. Stir in minced garlic and grated ginger. Sauté for an additional 2 minutes until fragrant.
3. Add curry powder, ground cumin, ground coriander, turmeric, and chili powder to the skillet. Cook for 1-2 minutes to toast the spices.
4. Add diced tomatoes, chickpeas, coconut milk, and tomato paste to the skillet. Season with salt and pepper. Bring to a simmer.
5. Simmer the curry for 15-20 minutes, stirring occasionally, until the flavors meld and the sauce thickens.
6. Adjust seasoning if needed.

For Cauliflower Rice:
7. In a separate skillet, heat olive oil over medium heat.
8. Add grated or processed cauliflower to the skillet. Sauté for 5-7 minutes or until the cauliflower is tender.
9. Season with salt and pepper.

Sesame Ginger Beef Stir-Fry with Quinoa

2 servings | 35 minutes

Cal 400
Fat 15 g
Carb 35 g
Protein 30 g
Sodium 600 mg
Potassium 500 mg
Phosphorus 250 mg

INGREDIENTS

For Sesame Ginger Beef:
- 1 pound beef sirloin or flank steak, thinly sliced
- 1/4 cup soy sauce (low-sodium)
- 2 tablespoons sesame oil
- 2 tablespoons rice vinegar
- 1 tablespoon honey or maple syrup
- 1 tablespoon ginger, grated
- 2 cloves garlic, minced
- 1 tablespoon cornstarch
- 2 tablespoons vegetable oil (for stir-frying)
- 1 cup broccoli florets
- 1 bell pepper, thinly sliced
- 1 carrot, julienned
- 1 cup snap peas, trimmed
- 2 green onions, sliced
- Sesame seeds for garnish

For Quinoa:
- 1 cup quinoa, uncooked
- 2 cups water
- 1/2 teaspoon salt

DIRECTIONS

For Quinoa:
1. Rinse quinoa under cold water.
2. In a saucepan, combine quinoa, water, and salt.
3. Bring to a boil, then reduce heat to low, cover, and simmer for 15-20 minutes or until the quinoa is cooked and water is absorbed.
4. Fluff the quinoa with a fork.

For Sesame Ginger Beef Stir-Fry:
1. In a bowl, whisk together soy sauce, sesame oil, rice vinegar, honey or maple syrup, grated ginger, minced garlic, and cornstarch.
2. Add thinly sliced beef to the marinade, ensuring it is well coated. Let it marinate for at least 15 minutes.
3. Heat vegetable oil in a wok or large skillet over high heat.
4. Add marinated beef to the hot wok and stir-fry for 2-3 minutes or until the beef is browned and cooked to your liking. Remove the beef from the wok and set aside.
5. In the same wok, add a bit more oil if needed. Stir-fry broccoli, bell pepper, julienned carrot, and snap peas for 3-5 minutes or until the vegetables are crisp-tender.
6. Add the cooked beef back to the wok and toss everything together.

Grilled Swordfish with Cucumber and Tomato Salad

2 servings | 35 minutes

Cal 350
Fat 20 g
Carb 15 g
Protein 30 g

Sodium 300 mg
Potassium 500 mg
Phosphorus 250 mg

INGREDIENTS

For Grilled Swordfish:
- 4 swordfish steaks (6 ounces each)
- 2 tablespoons olive oil
- Zest and juice of 1 lemon
- 2 cloves garlic, minced
- 1 teaspoon dried oregano
- Salt and pepper to taste

For Cucumber and Tomato Salad:
- 2 cucumbers, diced
- 2 cups cherry tomatoes, halved
- 1/4 cup red onion, thinly sliced
- 1/4 cup feta cheese, crumbled
- 2 tablespoons fresh dill, chopped
- 2 tablespoons red wine vinegar
- 2 tablespoons olive oil
- Salt and pepper to taste

DIRECTIONS

For Grilled Swordfish:
1. In a bowl, whisk together olive oil, lemon zest, lemon juice, minced garlic, dried oregano, salt, and pepper.
2. Place swordfish steaks in a shallow dish and pour the marinade over them. Let them marinate for at least 30 minutes.
3. Preheat the grill to medium-high heat.
4. Grill swordfish steaks for 4-5 minutes per side or until they are cooked through and have nice grill marks.

For Cucumber and Tomato Salad:
1. In a large bowl, combine diced cucumbers, cherry tomatoes, thinly sliced red onion, crumbled feta cheese, and chopped fresh dill.
2. In a small bowl, whisk together red wine vinegar, olive oil, salt, and pepper.
3. Pour the dressing over the cucumber and tomato mixture and toss gently to combine.

Vegetarian Lentil and Sweet Potato Stew

2 servings | 35 minutes

Cal 300
Fat 5 g
Carb 50 g
Protein 15 g

Sodium 400 mg
Potassium 700 mg
Phosphorus 250 mg

INGREDIENTS

- 1 cup dried green or brown lentils, rinsed and drained
- 2 sweet potatoes, peeled and diced
- 1 onion, chopped
- 2 carrots, sliced
- 2 celery stalks, chopped
- 3 cloves garlic, minced
- 1 can (14 ounces) diced tomatoes
- 4 cups vegetable broth (low-sodium)
- 1 teaspoon ground cumin
- 1 teaspoon ground coriander
- 1/2 teaspoon smoked paprika
- 1/2 teaspoon turmeric
- Salt and pepper to taste
- 2 tablespoons olive oil
- Fresh parsley for garnish (optional)

DIRECTIONS

1. In a large pot, heat olive oil over medium heat.
2. Add chopped onion and sauté until translucent.
3. Add minced garlic, ground cumin, ground coriander, smoked paprika, and turmeric to the pot. Cook for 1-2 minutes to toast the spices.
4. Stir in diced sweet potatoes, sliced carrots, and chopped celery. Cook for an additional 5 minutes.
5. Add rinsed lentils, diced tomatoes, and vegetable broth to the pot. Season with salt and pepper.
6. Bring the stew to a boil, then reduce heat to low, cover, and simmer for 25-30 minutes or until the lentils and sweet potatoes are tender.
7. Adjust seasoning if needed.
8. Serve hot, garnished with fresh parsley if desired.

Cilantro Lime Turkey Burger with Baked Sweet Potato Wedges

2 servings | 35 minutes

Cal 400
Fat 15 g
Carb 40 g
Protein 25 g
Sodium 400 mg
Potassium 500 mg
Phosphorus 250 mg

INGREDIENTS

For Cilantro Lime Turkey Burger:
- 1 pound ground turkey
- 1/4 cup breadcrumbs
- 1/4 cup fresh cilantro, chopped
- Zest and juice of 1 lime
- 2 cloves garlic, minced
- 1 teaspoon ground cumin
- Salt and pepper to taste
- Whole wheat burger buns
- Lettuce, tomato, and red onion for garnish

For Baked Sweet Potato Wedges:
- 2 large sweet potatoes, washed and cut into wedges
- 2 tablespoons olive oil
- 1 teaspoon smoked paprika
- 1/2 teaspoon garlic powder
- 1/2 teaspoon onion powder
- Salt and pepper to taste

DIRECTIONS

1. **For Cilantro Lime Turkey Burger:**
2. In a bowl, combine ground turkey, breadcrumbs, chopped cilantro, lime zest, lime juice, minced garlic, ground cumin, salt, and pepper.
3. Mix until well combined and form the mixture into burger patties.
4. Preheat a grill or grill pan over medium-high heat. Grill the turkey burgers for 5-6 minutes per side or until fully cooked.
5. Toast the whole wheat burger buns on the grill for a minute or until they have grill marks.
6. Assemble the burgers with lettuce, tomato, and red onion.
7. **For Baked Sweet Potato Wedges:**
8. Preheat the oven to 400°F (200°C).
9. In a large bowl, toss sweet potato wedges with olive oil, smoked paprika, garlic powder, onion powder, salt, and pepper.
10. Spread the sweet potato wedges in a single layer on a baking sheet.
11. Bake for 25-30 minutes or until the sweet potatoes are tender and golden brown.

Caprese Zucchini Noodles with Grilled Chicken

2 servings | 35 minutes

Cal 350
Fat 15 g
Carb 15 g
Protein 30 g
Sodium 400 mg
Potassium 600 mg
Phosphorus 300 mg

INGREDIENTS

For Grilled Chicken:
- 4 boneless, skinless chicken breasts
- 2 tablespoons olive oil
- 2 cloves garlic, minced
- 1 teaspoon dried oregano
- Salt and pepper to taste

For Caprese Zucchini Noodles:
- 4 medium zucchini, spiralized into noodles
- 1 cup cherry tomatoes, halved
- 1 cup fresh mozzarella, diced
- 1/4 cup fresh basil, chopped
- 2 tablespoons balsamic glaze
- 2 tablespoons olive oil
- Salt and pepper to taste

DIRECTIONS

1. **For Grilled Chicken:**
2. In a bowl, mix olive oil, minced garlic, dried oregano, salt, and pepper.
3. Place chicken breasts in a shallow dish and coat them with the marinade. Let them marinate for at least 30 minutes.
4. Preheat the grill to medium-high heat. Grill the chicken for 6-8 minutes per side or until fully cooked.
5. **For Caprese Zucchini Noodles:**
6. In a large skillet, heat olive oil over medium heat. Add spiralized zucchini noodles and sauté for 2-3 minutes or until they are just tender.
7. In a bowl, toss together zucchini noodles, cherry tomatoes, fresh mozzarella, chopped fresh basil, balsamic glaze, olive oil, salt, and pepper.
8. Divide the zucchini noodle mixture among plates.
9. Slice the grilled chicken and place it on top of the zucchini noodles.

Teriyaki Salmon with Quinoa and Steamed Spinach

2 servings 35 minutes

Cal 400
Fat 15 g
Carb 35 g
Protein 30 g
Sodium 500 mg
Potassium 600 mg
Phosphorus 250 mg

INGREDIENTS

For Teriyaki Salmon:
- 4 salmon fillets
- 1/4 cup low-sodium soy sauce
- 2 tablespoons honey or maple syrup
- 1 tablespoon rice vinegar
- 1 tablespoon sesame oil
- 2 cloves garlic, minced
- 1 teaspoon ginger, grated
- Sesame seeds for garnish
- Sliced green onions for garnish

For Quinoa:
- 1 cup quinoa, uncooked
- 2 cups water
- 1/2 teaspoon salt

For Steamed Spinach:
- 4 cups fresh spinach, washed and trimmed
- 1 tablespoon olive oil
- 1 clove garlic, minced
- Salt and pepper to taste

DIRECTIONS

1. **For Teriyaki Salmon:**
2. In a bowl, whisk together low-sodium soy sauce, honey or maple syrup, rice vinegar, sesame oil, minced garlic, and grated ginger.
3. Place salmon fillets in a shallow dish and pour the teriyaki marinade over them. Let them marinate for at least 30 minutes.
4. Preheat the oven to 400°F (200°C).
5. Transfer marinated salmon fillets to a baking sheet lined with parchment paper. Bake for 12-15 minutes or until the salmon is cooked through.
6. Sprinkle sesame seeds and sliced green onions over the cooked salmon.
7. **For Quinoa:**
8. Rinse quinoa under cold water.
9. In a saucepan, combine quinoa, water, and salt.
10. Bring to a boil, then reduce heat to low, cover, and simmer for 15-20 minutes or until the quinoa is cooked and water is absorbed.
11. Fluff the quinoa with a fork.
12. **For Steamed Spinach:**
13. In a large skillet, heat olive oil over medium heat. Add minced garlic and sauté until fragrant.
14. Add fresh spinach to the skillet and toss until wilted. Season with salt and pepper.

Chicken and Vegetable Skillet with Quinoa

2 servings | 35 minutes

Cal 350
Fat 10 g
Carb 40 g
Protein 25 g
Sodium 400 mg
Potassium 500 mg
Phosphorus 250 mg

INGREDIENTS

For Chicken and Vegetable Skillet:
- 1 pound boneless, skinless chicken breasts, cut into bite-sized pieces
- 2 tablespoons olive oil
- 1 onion, diced
- 2 bell peppers (any color), sliced
- 1 zucchini, sliced
- 1 cup cherry tomatoes, halved
- 2 cloves garlic, minced
- 1 teaspoon dried oregano
- 1 teaspoon dried thyme
- Salt and pepper to taste
- Fresh parsley for garnish (optional)

For Quinoa:
- 1 cup quinoa, uncooked
- 2 cups water
- 1/2 teaspoon salt

DIRECTIONS

For Quinoa:
1. Rinse quinoa under cold water.
2. In a saucepan, combine quinoa, water, and salt.
3. Bring to a boil, then reduce heat to low, cover, and simmer for 15-20 minutes or until the quinoa is cooked and water is absorbed.
4. Fluff the quinoa with a fork.

For Chicken and Vegetable Skillet:
5. In a large skillet, heat olive oil over medium-high heat.
6. Add diced onion and sauté until translucent.
7. Add bite-sized chicken pieces to the skillet and cook until browned and cooked through.
8. Stir in sliced bell peppers, sliced zucchini, cherry tomatoes, minced garlic, dried oregano, dried thyme, salt, and pepper. Cook for an additional 5-7 minutes or until the vegetables are tender.
9. Adjust seasoning if needed.

Roasted Red Pepper and Lentil Soup with Whole Wheat Bread

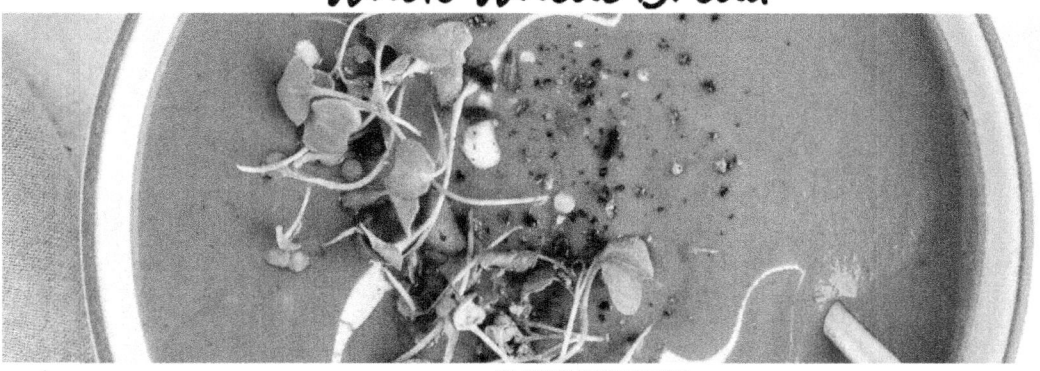

2 servings | **35 minutes**

Cal 300
Fat 15 g
Carb 45 g
Protein 15 g
Sodium 500 mg
Potassium 600 mg
Phosphorus 250 mg

INGREDIENTS

For Roasted Red Pepper and Lentil Soup:
- 1 cup red lentils, rinsed and drained
- 2 large red bell peppers, roasted and peeled
- 1 onion, chopped
- 2 cloves garlic, minced
- 1 can (14 ounces) diced tomatoes (low-sodium)
- 4 cups vegetable broth (low-sodium)
- 1 teaspoon ground cumin
- 1 teaspoon smoked paprika
- 1/2 teaspoon red pepper flakes (optional, for heat)
- Salt and pepper to taste
- 2 tablespoons olive oil
- Fresh parsley for garnish (optional)
- Greek yogurt for topping (optional)

For Whole Wheat Bread:
- 4 slices whole wheat bread

DIRECTIONS

For Roasted Red Pepper and Lentil Soup:
1. Preheat the oven to 400°F (200°C).
2. Place red bell peppers on a baking sheet and roast in the oven for 20-25 minutes or until the skins are charred.
3. Remove peppers from the oven, place them in a bowl, and cover with a lid or plastic wrap. Let them steam for 10 minutes.
4. Peel the skins off the roasted peppers, remove seeds, and chop them.
5. In a large pot, heat olive oil over medium heat. Add chopped onion and sauté until translucent.
6. Add minced garlic and sauté for an additional 2 minutes.
7. Stir in red lentils, diced roasted red peppers, diced tomatoes, vegetable broth, ground cumin, smoked paprika, red pepper flakes (if using), salt, and pepper.
8. Bring the soup to a boil, then reduce heat to low, cover, and simmer for 20-25 minutes or until the lentils are tender.
9. Adjust seasoning if needed.

For Whole Wheat Bread:
1. Toast the whole wheat bread slices in a toaster or oven until they are golden brown.

Mediterranean Stuffed Acorn Squash with Ground Turkey

2 servings | 50 minutes

Cal 400
Fat 15 g
Carb 45 g
Protein 25 g
Sodium 400 mg
Potassium 700 mg
Phosphorus 250 mg

INGREDIENTS

For Stuffed Acorn Squash:
- 2 acorn squash, halved and seeds removed
- 1 pound ground turkey
- 1 tablespoon olive oil
- 1 onion, finely chopped
- 2 cloves garlic, minced
- 1 teaspoon dried oregano
- 1 teaspoon dried thyme
- 1 teaspoon ground cumin
- 1 cup cherry tomatoes, halved
- 1/2 cup Kalamata olives, sliced
- 1/2 cup crumbled feta cheese
- Salt and pepper to taste
- Fresh parsley for garnish

DIRECTIONS

1. Preheat the oven to 400°F (200°C).
2. Place halved acorn squash on a baking sheet, cut side down. Bake for 30-40 minutes or until the squash is tender when pierced with a fork.
3. While the squash is baking, heat olive oil in a skillet over medium heat. Add chopped onion and sauté until translucent.
4. Add minced garlic and ground turkey to the skillet. Cook until the turkey is browned and cooked through.
5. Stir in dried oregano, dried thyme, ground cumin, cherry tomatoes, and Kalamata olives. Cook for an additional 5 minutes until the tomatoes are softened.
6. Season the turkey mixture with salt and pepper. Remove from heat.
7. Once the acorn squash halves are done baking, flip them over and fill each half with the ground turkey mixture.
8. Top each stuffed squash with crumbled feta cheese.
9. Return the stuffed squash to the oven and bake for an additional 10-15 minutes or until the feta is melted and bubbly.
10. Garnish with fresh parsley.

Greek Lemon Chicken with Roasted Vegetables

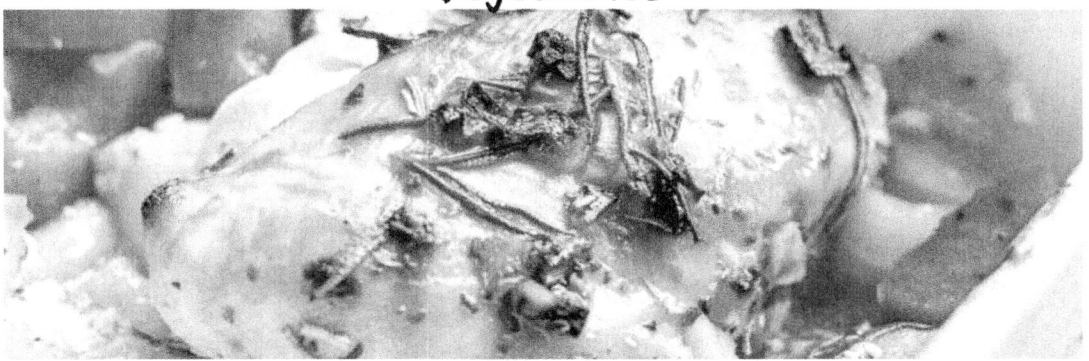

2 servings | 50 minutes

Cal 350
Fat 15 g
Carb 25 g
Protein 30 g
Sodium 400 mg
Potassium 600 mg
Phosphorus 250 mg

INGREDIENTS

For Greek Lemon Chicken:
- 4 boneless, skinless chicken breasts
- 1/4 cup olive oil
- Zest and juice of 2 lemons
- 3 cloves garlic, minced
- 1 teaspoon dried oregano
- 1 teaspoon dried thyme
- Salt and pepper to taste
- Fresh parsley for garnish

For Roasted Vegetables:
- 1 large red bell pepper, sliced
- 1 large yellow bell pepper, sliced
- 1 red onion, sliced
- 1 zucchini, sliced
- 1 cup cherry tomatoes, halved
- 2 tablespoons olive oil
- 1 teaspoon dried oregano
- Salt and pepper to taste

DIRECTIONS

For Greek Lemon Chicken:
1. Preheat the oven to 400°F (200°C).
2. In a bowl, whisk together olive oil, lemon zest, lemon juice, minced garlic, dried oregano, dried thyme, salt, and pepper.
3. Place chicken breasts in a shallow dish and coat them with the lemon marinade. Let them marinate for at least 30 minutes.
4. Heat a skillet over medium-high heat. Sear the chicken breasts for 2-3 minutes on each side until golden brown.
5. Transfer the seared chicken to a baking dish and bake in the preheated oven for 20-25 minutes or until the chicken is cooked through.
6. Garnish with fresh parsley.

For Roasted Vegetables:
7. In a large bowl, toss together sliced red bell pepper, sliced yellow bell pepper, sliced red onion, sliced zucchini, cherry tomatoes, olive oil, dried oregano, salt, and pepper.
8. Spread the vegetable mixture on a baking sheet.
9. Roast in the oven for 20-25 minutes or until the vegetables are tender and slightly caramelized.

Quinoa and Chickpea Stuffed Eggplant

2 servings | 50 minutes

Cal 350
Fat 10 g
Carb 55 g
Protein 15 g
Sodium 400 mg
Potassium 800 mg
Phosphorus 250 mg

INGREDIENTS

- 2 large eggplants, halved lengthwise
- 1 cup quinoa, uncooked
- 2 cups vegetable broth (low-sodium)
- 1 can (15 ounces) chickpeas, drained and rinsed
- 1 red bell pepper, diced
- 1 yellow bell pepper, diced
- 1 red onion, finely chopped
- 2 cloves garlic, minced
- 1 teaspoon ground cumin
- 1 teaspoon smoked paprika
- 1/2 teaspoon ground coriander
- Salt and pepper to taste
- 2 tablespoons olive oil
- Fresh parsley for garnish

DIRECTIONS

1. Preheat the oven to 400°F (200°C).
2. Scoop out the flesh from the halved eggplants, leaving a 1/2-inch border. Chop the scooped-out eggplant flesh and set aside.
3. In a saucepan, combine quinoa and vegetable broth. Bring to a boil, then reduce heat to low, cover, and simmer for 15-20 minutes or until the quinoa is cooked and water is absorbed.
4. In a large skillet, heat olive oil over medium heat. Add chopped red onion and sauté until translucent.
5. Add minced garlic, chopped eggplant flesh, diced red bell pepper, diced yellow bell pepper, and sauté for an additional 5 minutes.
6. Stir in cooked quinoa, chickpeas, ground cumin, smoked paprika, ground coriander, salt, and pepper. Cook for an additional 5 minutes until the mixture is well combined.
7. Place the hollowed-out eggplant halves on a baking sheet.
8. Fill each eggplant half with the quinoa and chickpea mixture.
9. Bake in the preheated oven for 25-30 minutes or until the eggplant is tender.
10. Garnish with fresh parsley before serving.

Shrimp and Asparagus Risotto with Parmesan

2 servings | 30 minutes

Cal 400
Fat 15 g
Carb 45 g
Protein 20 g
Sodium 500 mg
Potassium 300 mg
Phosphorus 200 mg

INGREDIENTS

- 1 pound medium shrimp, peeled and deveined
- 1 bunch asparagus, trimmed and cut into bite-sized pieces
- 1 1/2 cups Arborio rice
- 1/2 cup dry white wine
- 4 cups low-sodium chicken or vegetable broth, warmed
- 1 onion, finely chopped
- 3 cloves garlic, minced
- 1/2 cup grated Parmesan cheese
- 2 tablespoons olive oil
- 1 tablespoon unsalted butter
- 1 teaspoon lemon zest
- Salt and pepper to taste
- Fresh parsley for garnish

DIRECTIONS

1. In a large skillet, heat 1 tablespoon of olive oil over medium heat. Add the shrimp and cook until they turn pink, about 2-3 minutes per side. Remove the shrimp from the skillet and set aside.
2. In the same skillet, add the remaining 1 tablespoon of olive oil. Sauté the chopped onion and minced garlic until softened.
3. Add Arborio rice to the skillet and stir to coat the rice with the oil and onions. Toast the rice for 2-3 minutes until it becomes translucent around the edges.
4. Pour in the white wine and cook until it is mostly absorbed, stirring frequently.
5. Begin adding the warmed broth, one ladle at a time, stirring constantly and allowing the liquid to be absorbed before adding more. Continue this process until the rice is creamy and cooked to al dente, about 18-20 minutes.
6. During the last 5 minutes of cooking, add the asparagus to the risotto. Continue to stir and cook until the asparagus is tender.
7. Stir in the cooked shrimp, grated Parmesan cheese, unsalted butter, and lemon zest. Season with salt and pepper to taste.
8. Remove the risotto from heat and let it rest for a minute before serving.
9. Garnish with fresh parsley.

Cabbage and White Bean Stir-Fry with Tofu

2 servings | 15 minutes

Cal 350
Fat 15 g
Carb 40 g
Protein 20 g
Sodium 400 mg
Potassium 500 mg
Phosphorus 300 mg

INGREDIENTS

For Stir-Fry:
- 1 block (14 ounces) extra-firm tofu, pressed and cubed
- 4 cups green cabbage, thinly sliced
- 1 can (15 ounces) white beans, drained and rinsed
- 1 red bell pepper, thinly sliced
- 1 carrot, julienned
- 3 green onions, sliced
- 3 cloves garlic, minced
- 1 tablespoon ginger, grated
- 2 tablespoons low-sodium soy sauce
- 1 tablespoon sesame oil
- 1 tablespoon rice vinegar
- 1 tablespoon hoisin sauce
- 1 teaspoon Sriracha sauce (optional, for heat)
- 2 tablespoons vegetable oil for stir-frying
- Sesame seeds for garnish

For Serving:
- Cooked brown rice or quinoa

DIRECTIONS

1. Press the tofu to remove excess water, then cut it into cubes.
2. Heat 1 tablespoon of vegetable oil in a large wok or skillet over medium-high heat. Add the tofu cubes and stir-fry until golden brown on all sides. Remove tofu from the pan and set aside.
3. In the same pan, add the remaining tablespoon of vegetable oil. Sauté minced garlic and grated ginger until fragrant.
4. Add sliced cabbage, julienned carrot, and sliced red bell pepper to the pan. Stir-fry for 3-4 minutes until the vegetables are slightly tender.
5. Stir in the cooked tofu, white beans, and sliced green onions.
6. In a small bowl, mix together low-sodium soy sauce, sesame oil, rice vinegar, hoisin sauce, and Sriracha sauce (if using).
7. Pour the sauce over the stir-fry and toss everything together until well coated. Cook for an additional 2-3 minutes.
8. Adjust the seasoning if needed.
9. Serve the stir-fry over cooked brown rice or quinoa.
10. Garnish with sesame seeds.

Smoothies

Berry Blast Smoothie

2 servings | 8 minutes

Cal 150
Fat 2 g
Carb 30 g
Protein 4 g

Sodium 30 mg
Potassium 200 mg
Phosphorus 50 mg

INGREDIENTS

- 1/2 cup blueberries (fresh or frozen)
- 1/2 cup strawberries (fresh or frozen)
- 1/2 cup raspberries (fresh or frozen)
- 1 small banana
- 1/2 cup low-potassium yogurt
- 1/2 cup water or almond milk

DIRECTIONS

1. If using frozen berries, allow them to thaw slightly for a few minutes.
2. In a blender, combine blueberries, strawberries, raspberries, bananas, low-potassium yogurt, and water or almond milk.
3. Blend on high speed until the mixture is smooth and well combined.
4. Taste the smoothie and adjust sweetness or thickness by adding more water or almond milk if needed.
5. Pour the smoothie into a glass and serve immediately.

Peachy Green Smoothie

2 servings | 8 minutes

Cal 120
Fat 4 g
Carb 20 g
Protein 5 g

Sodium 40 mg
Potassium 250 mg
Phosphorus 60 mg

INGREDIENTS
- 1/2 cup peaches (fresh or frozen)
- 1 cup baby spinach
- 1/2 cup cucumber, peeled and sliced
- 1/2 cup low-potassium yogurt
- 1 tablespoon chia seeds
- 1/2 cup water or coconut water

DIRECTIONS
1. If using frozen peaches, allow them to thaw slightly for a few minutes.
2. In a blender, combine peaches, baby spinach, cucumber, low-potassium yogurt, chia seeds, and water or coconut water.
3. Blend on high speed until the mixture is smooth and well combined.
4. Taste the smoothie and adjust sweetness or thickness by adding more water or coconut water if needed.
5. Pour the smoothie into a glass and serve immediately.

Cucumber Mint Cooler

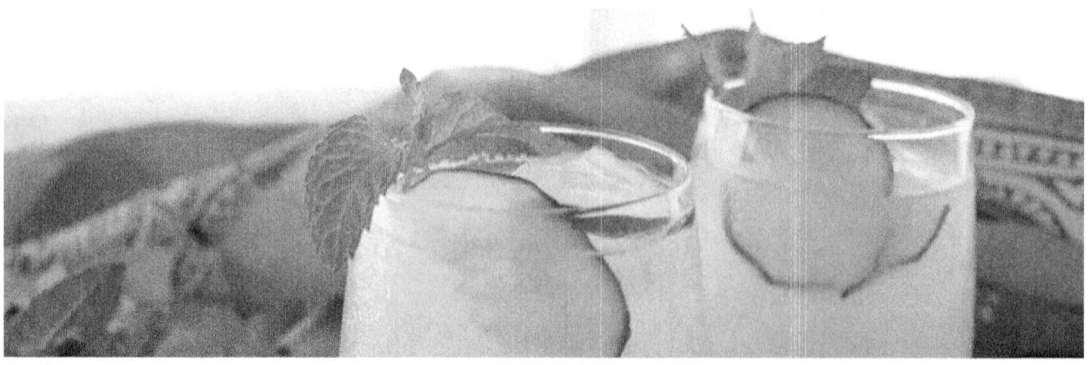

2 servings | 8 minutes

Cal 90
Fat 3 g
Carb 15 g
Protein 4 g

Sodium 30 mg
Potassium 180 mg
Phosphorus 60 mg

INGREDIENTS

- 1/2 cucumber, peeled and sliced
- 1/2 cup fresh mint leaves
- 1/2 cup honeydew melon
- 1 tablespoon flaxseeds
- 1/2 cup low-potassium yogurt
- 1/2 cup water or green tea

DIRECTIONS

1. In a blender, combine cucumber slices, fresh mint leaves, honeydew melon, flaxseeds, low-potassium yogurt, and water or green tea.
2. Blend on high speed until the mixture is smooth and well combined.
3. Taste the cooler and adjust sweetness or thickness by adding more water or green tea if needed.
4. Optionally, strain the mixture using a fine mesh strainer to remove any pulp.
5. Pour the cooler into a glass over ice and garnish with a mint sprig.

Cherry Almond Delight

2 servings | 8 minutes

Cal 200
Fat 10 g
Carb 20 g
Protein 6 g

Sodium 40 mg
Potassium 180 mg
Phosphorus 80 mg

INGREDIENTS
- 1/2 cup cherries (fresh or frozen)
- 1 tablespoon almond butter
- 1/2 cup low-potassium yogurt
- 1 tablespoon hemp seeds
- 1/2 cup water or almond milk

DIRECTIONS
1. If using frozen cherries, allow them to thaw slightly for a few minutes.
2. In a blender, combine cherries, almond butter, low-potassium yogurt, hemp seeds, and water or almond milk.
3. Blend on high speed until the mixture is smooth and well combined.
4. Taste the delight and adjust sweetness or thickness by adding more water or almond milk if needed.
5. Pour the delight into a glass and serve immediately.

Citrus Berry Fusion

2 servings 8 minutes

Cal 120
Fat 3 g
Carb 20 g
Protein 4 g

Sodium 30 mg
Potassium 200 mg
Phosphorus 50 mg

INGREDIENTS

- 1/2 cup mixed berries (blueberries, strawberries, raspberries)
- 1/2 orange, peeled
- 1/2 cup low-potassium yogurt
- 1 tablespoon flaxseeds
- 1/2 cup water or orange juice (diluted)

DIRECTIONS

1. If using frozen berries, allow them to thaw slightly for a few minutes.
2. In a blender, combine mixed berries, peeled orange, low-potassium yogurt, flaxseeds, and water or diluted orange juice.
3. Blend on high speed until the mixture is smooth and well combined.
4. Taste the fusion and adjust sweetness or thickness by adding more water or diluted orange juice if needed.
5. Pour the fusion into a glass and serve immediately.

Vanilla Date Smoothie

2 servings | 8 minutes

Cal 180
Fat 2 g
Carb 35 g
Protein 5 g
Sodium 40 mg
Potassium 220 mg
Phosphorus 70 mg

INGREDIENTS
- 2 dates, pitted
- 1/2 teaspoon vanilla extract
- 1/2 cup low-potassium yogurt
- 1/2 banana
- 1/2 cup water or rice milk

DIRECTIONS
1. In a blender, combine pitted dates, vanilla extract, low-potassium yogurt, banana, and water or rice milk.
2. Blend on high speed until the mixture is smooth and well combined.
3. Taste the smoothie and adjust sweetness or thickness by adding more water or rice milk if needed.
4. Pour the smoothie into a glass and serve immediately.

Apple Cinnamon Spice Smoothie

2 servings | 8 minutes

Cal 130
Fat 4 g
Carb 25 g
Protein 4 g

Sodium 30 mg
Potassium 180 mg
Phosphorus 70 mg

INGREDIENTS

- 1/2 apple, cored and sliced
- 1/2 teaspoon ground cinnamon
- 1/2 cup low-potassium yogurt
- 1 tablespoon chia seeds
- 1/2 cup water or diluted apple juice

DIRECTIONS

1. In a blender, combine apple slices, ground cinnamon, low-potassium yogurt, chia seeds, and water or diluted apple juice.
2. Blend on high speed until the mixture is smooth and well combined.
3. Taste the smoothie and adjust sweetness or thickness by adding more water or diluted apple juice if needed.
4. Pour the smoothie into a glass and serve immediately.

Mango Avocado Dream Smoothie

2 servings | 8 minutes

Cal 200
Fat 5 g
Carb 25 g
Protein 5 g

Sodium 30 mg
Potassium 300 mg
Phosphorus 70 mg

INGREDIENTS
- 1/2 cup mango chunks (fresh or frozen)
- 1/4 avocado
- 1/2 cup low-potassium yogurt
- 1 tablespoon pumpkin seeds
- 1/2 cup water or coconut water

DIRECTIONS
1. If using frozen mango chunks, allow them to thaw slightly for a few minutes.
2. In a blender, combine mango chunks, peeled and pitted avocado, low-potassium yogurt, pumpkin seeds, and water or coconut water.
3. Blend on high speed until the mixture is smooth and well combined.
4. Taste the smoothie and adjust sweetness or thickness by adding more water or coconut water if needed.
5. Pour the smoothie into a glass and serve immediately.

Pineapple Ginger Zing Smoothie

2 servings | 8 minutes

Cal 130
Fat 4 g
Carb 20 g
Protein 4 g

Sodium 30 mg
Potassium 220 mg
Phosphorus 60 mg

INGREDIENTS
- 1/2 cup pineapple chunks
- 1/2 teaspoon grated ginger
- 1/2 cup low-potassium yogurt
- 1 tablespoon chia seeds
- 1/2 cup water or diluted pineapple juice

DIRECTIONS
1. In a blender, combine pineapple chunks, grated ginger, low-potassium yogurt, chia seeds, and water or diluted pineapple juice.
2. Blend on high speed until the mixture is smooth and well combined.
3. Taste the smoothie and adjust sweetness or thickness by adding more water or diluted pineapple juice if needed.
4. Pour the smoothie into a glass and serve immediately.

Blueberry Basil Bliss

2 servings   8 minutes

Cal 120
Fat 3 g
Carb 20 g
Protein 4 g

Sodium 30 mg
Potassium 180 mg
Phosphorus 50 mg

INGREDIENTS

- 1/2 cup blueberries (fresh or frozen)
- 1 tablespoon fresh basil leaves
- 1/2 cup low-potassium yogurt
- 1 tablespoon flaxseeds
- 1/2 cup water or almond milk

DIRECTIONS

1. If using frozen blueberries, allow them to thaw slightly for a few minutes.
2. In a blender, combine blueberries, fresh basil leaves, low-potassium yogurt, flaxseeds, and water or almond milk.
3. Blend on high speed until the mixture is smooth and well combined.
4. Taste the smoothie and adjust sweetness or thickness by adding more water or almond milk if needed.
5. Pour the smoothie into a glass and serve immediately.

Conclusion

At the end of this enlightening manual, it is clear that following a professionally designed nutrition plan is essential to kidney health and not just something to recommend. It is impossible to overestimate the significance of these dietary interventions, as they are fundamental to the management of renal disease and the promotion of general health.

By embracing a kidney-friendly nutrition plan, individuals can proactively address key aspects of kidney health. Through the regulation of sodium, potassium, phosphorus, and protein intake, individuals can mitigate the strain on their kidneys, slow down the progression of kidney disease, and enhance their quality of life.

The wisdom shared throughout this guide underscores the necessity of personalized care, emphasizing the significance of consulting with a registered dietitian specializing in kidney health. Education plays a pivotal role, enabling individuals to make informed choices, read labels discerningly, and cultivate a deeper understanding of their nutritional needs.

Practical advice, such as meal planning, staying hydrated within prescribed limits, and vigilant monitoring of lab results, empowers individuals to take charge of their kidney health. This journey is not without challenges, but with commitment, education, and a collaborative effort with healthcare professionals, it is a journey that can lead to profound improvements in health outcomes.

In essence, this guide serves as a beacon of knowledge and guidance, encouraging individuals to see their nutrition plan not as a restrictive measure but as a powerful tool for wellness. Sticking to a kidney diet is an investment in one's health, a commitment that opens avenues to a healthier, more vibrant life. As we conclude this exploration, let it be a catalyst for positive change and a testament to the transformative impact that a well-managed nutrition plan can have on the journey to kidney health.

2024

Jasmine Patel

Printed in Great Britain
by Amazon